LIVING
The Life of
GOD

JAMES MILLER

ISBN
978-1-958690-81-9 (Paperback)
978-1-958690-82-6 (eBook)
978-1-958690-88-8 (Hardcover)

Dedication

I dedicate this book to the kingdom of God and the family at Grace Assembly of God who allow me to be their pastor. And to my wife Judy and my children, James, Michael, Christopher, Jessica, Kevin, and Joshua.

ACKNOWLEDGMENT

First and foremost, I would like to express my sincerest gratitude for the accomplishment of my book to Quantum Discovery. This company has entrusted me to a committed team that encourages me to continue working on my piece.

This project would not have been possible without Grace Winters, my literary agent, that encourages me to have my book re-publish. Her pitch about my book ignites my writing career.

I would like to recognize the invaluable assistance of Alex Morgan, my Project Manager. His prompt responses gave me the impression that they are interested to work with me and my book.

And lastly, I would like to extend my deepest gratitude to the Fulfillment Team and their book designer, Elvis Payne. Elvis and his team have crafted my book cover with their in-depth skills in this art. My book is exceptionally great!

TABLE OF CONTENTS

ABOUT THE AUTHOR

Jim is Senior Pastor of Grace Assembly of God in Hephzibah, Georgia. He retired from the U. S. Army in August 1989, after twenty one years of service, with the highest rank of First Sergeant. He retired again from Serta Mattress in Grovetown, Georgia in 2011 after serving for 10 years as the Plant Administrator.

He is married to Judy who helped him raise six children, of which, one has gone on to be with the Lord. He has an accounting degree from Ashworth, College, as well ordination credentials with the Assemblies of God denomination through the Berean Ministry Studies, which were acquired while in the military. He wrote one of the Plumbing SQT manual for the military in 1982 with a team of other writers and also put the finishes touches on the Army construction manual at that time.

Jim and his wife, Judy live in Augusta, Georgia. (706) 796-3810. jimmiller232@gmail.com.

PREFACE

This exposition on the statement concerning the life of God in Ephesians 4: 18, is being written because I believe the life of God is misunderstood by some to just mean the eternal life of God. Living the life of God leads to an abundance of well being. First, we have the promise of eternal life. Second, this life when lived attracts good health, good relationships, and prosperity and success in whatever goals we set in life. His nature evolving in us leads to finding the "Abundant Life" Jesus speaks of in John 10: 10. This life is an adventure in attracting good success in all areas of life and living a life of significance. When His virtuous nature becomes our nature, we begin to reap good things, experiencing well being like a river as mentioned above and affirmed in Isaiah 48: 18.

No one ever hated a person full of love, joy, peace, longsuffering, kindness, goodness, faith, gentleness, and self-control, unless they were warped. People with these virtues live a life of energy, vitality, and radiate peace and joy. John said "Beloved, I pray that you may prosper in all things and be in health, just as your soul prospers." 3 John 2. The spirit of man grows just like the body when given the proper diet, 1 Timothy 4: 14 – 16. By the teaching and help of the Holy Spirit we are changed into this likeness and image, 2 Corinthians 3: 18.

To help us get to this place in our character and nature, St Paul prayed that we would receive discernment into the His virtues that are excellent and honorable, see Philippians 1: 9

– 10. When we begin to discern the excellent and adapt to its' virtuous wisdom for living life, by meditating on His word and applying it, then we become like him. As we become established in the habits of things that are excellent, we become a fragrance of Him, (See 2 Corinthians 2: 14 – 16, 2 Corinthians 3: 18 and Proverbs 4: 23 – 27).

Discernment is acquired by due diligence and on purpose by meditating on these things of excellence. Paul asserts the spirit of man needs a diet consisting of this, "Finally brethren, whatever things are true, whatever things that are noble, whatever things are just, whatever things that are pure, whatever things are lovely, whatever things are of good report, if there is any virtue, and if there is anything praiseworthy – meditate on these things." Paul said in Philippians 4: 8, NKJV.

Peter tells us how to attain it this way, "Grace and peace be multiplied to you in the knowledge of God and of Jesus our Lord, as His divine power has given to us all things that pertain to life and godliness, through the knowledge of Him who called us to glory and virtue, by which have been given to us exceedingly great and precious promises, that through these you may be partakers of the divine nature, having escaped the corruption that is in the world through lust. But also for this very reason giving all diligence, add to your faith virtue, to virtue knowledge, to knowledge self control, to self control, perseverance, to perseverance godliness, to godliness brotherly kindness, and to brotherly kindness love. For if these things are yours and abound, you will be neither barren nor unfruitful in the knowledge of our Lord Jesus Christ. For he who lacks these things is shortsighted, even to blindness, and has forgotten that, he was cleansed from his old sins. Therefore, brethren, be even more diligent to make your calling and election sure, for if you do these things you will never stumble; for so an entrance will be supplied to you abundantly into the everlasting kingdom of our Lord and Savior Jesus Christ." 2 Peter 1: 2 – 11, NKJV.

As we meditate on God's word, apply and pray, we begin to make the transformation. Let us strive to be perfect and complete His in His will – His life in us - His will for us. See Colossians 4: 12.

My hope is this reading will be a time that promotes growth in the grace and knowledge of God for us all.

In His Name

Jim

CHAPTER I

"THE LIFE OF GOD"

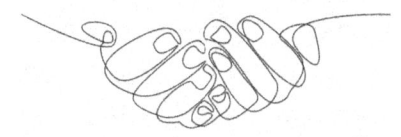

They are darkened in their understanding and separated from the life of God, because of the ignorance that is in them due to the hardening of their hearts.

Ephesians 4: 18, NIV.

What is the life of God, that this portion of scripture is talking of? Is it eternal life or His virtues? It can be both, eternal life and His virtues, but mainly the virtues and Godly principles that make up the Holy character of God. From verse 17 through verse 24 Paul is talking of a transition that has to take place. And thank God we don't have to do it on our own. Christians are called by God to a Holy Life " Because it is written, Be ye holy; for I am holy," 1 Peter 1: 16, KJV. Holiness means wholesome. Wholesomeness is His nature. "This then is the message which we have heard of him and declare unto you that God is light and in him is no darkness at all." 1 John 1: 5, KJV. There is nothing unclean or unwholesome in God, nor can be he be tempted by it nor does he tempt men with it. See James 1: 13.

The life we are to live, taught by the Spirit and mentored by Jesus Christ in the scriptures, is a life that imitates God, (See Ephesians 5:1-2). Paul says it is a new life style for us, "... even so we also should walk in newness of life" Romans 6: 4, KJV. This life is a mindset that is taught by the Holy Spirit, thus the terminology, "To be Spiritually Minded" or to have the mind set on the things of the Spirit will lead to life and peace, as found in Romans 8: 5 – 6, KJV. Moreover, if learned and adhered to, it renders a person a harvest of peace as spoken of in Romans 8: 6 and Isaiah 48: 18. This is what Jesus meant calling it an "Abundant Life", alluded to in John 10: 10.

It is a life-style of godly principles based on love, truth, and continuous holiness *(wholesomeness)* and integrity. It renders an individual wholesome and harmless. This is the image of God, and it is the intention of God for all of mankind to have by applying His principles in conducting all our affairs on earth. We become what we think and do. It becomes a life free from fear and anxiety because a spiritual mind thinks no harm towards his neighbor. The spiritual mindset will only do good and not evil, therefore has an easy conscience. A French proverb goes like this, "There is no softer pillow than an easy conscience."

A carnal mindset will drain an individual of vitality because of its' negativity towards people and circumstances. The spiritual mindset gives positive energy due to its' positive mindset. We see this in the life we live because it is expressed in our environment due to this mindset, either carnal or spiritual (See Romans 2: 8 – 11 & 8: 6).

The teaching and the philosophy of the life of Jesus Christ, produces the mindset of the Spirit and is expressed by being, full of love, joy, peace, patience, kindness, goodness, faithfulness, gentleness, and self control, as asserted to in Galatians 5: 22. These attitudes are the things that are excellent and honorable concerning the character and personality of God that Paul prayed we would be able to discern, see Philippians 1: 9 – 10.

Paul also said they are spiritually discerned in another place. "...
But the natural man does not receiveth the things of the Spirit
of God, for they are foolishness unto him; neither can he know
them, because they are spiritually discerned," 1 Corinthians 2:
10 – 14, KJV.

Paul stated the condition of the ignorant or reprobate mind.
It causes this separation from the understanding of the life of
God. They have a mind and heart that they have hardened,
through stubbornness, and cannot receive the teaching of the
truth from the Spirit. This is due to the willful ignorance in
them (See Ephesians 4: 17 – 18, NIV), and spoken of in Romans
1: 21 – 28.

This mind thinks that the things of God are foolishness and
foolish to learn, 1 Corinthians 2: 14. The natural man is the
carnal man; the Spirit has not regenerated the spirit, mind, and
heart of the carnal man. Therefore, it has a hatred toward the
things of God, (See James 4: 4, NIV). It reveals this hostility
by opposition, scoffing at, and displays a refusal to practice
godliness. Thus, being hostile to the life style God intended for
man. We see this in the effort to erase Christianity from public
view, along with the abortion, homosexual agenda, and the
limiting Christian speech today. They refuse to acknowledge
the truth about God and set their own morality standards of
tolerance.

This should not be a suprise to us because it is foretold in
scripture:

This know also, that in the last days perilous times shall
come. For men shall be lovers of their own selves, covetous,
boasters, proud, blasphemers, disobedient to parents, unthankful,
unholy, without natural affection, trucebreakers, false accusers,
incontinent, fierce, despisers of those that are good,, traitors,
heady, highminded, lovers of pleasures more than lovers of God;

Having a form of godliness, but denying the power thereof; from such turn away.

2 Timothy 3: 1 – 5, KJV.

This is due to a lack of discernment as stated above in 1 Corinthians 2: 10 – 14. We are called to discernment in 1 John 4: 2, John and James lacked good spiritual discernment as we see in Luke 9: 51 – 56, when they wanted to call down fire on the Samaritan village that refused them lodging. Jesus informed them, "... Ye know what manner of spirit you are of." in verse 55, KJV. And Paul exhorted us with this warning in 1 Timothy:

"Now the Spirit speaketh expressly, that in the latter times some shall depart from the faith, giving heed to seducing spirits and doctrines of devils."

1 Timothy 4: 1, KJV.

Then he gives an examples of this happening in Christians in chapter 5: "But the younger widows refuse: for when they have begun to wax wanton against Christ they will be marry;... For some are already turned aside after Satan", 1 Timothy 5: 11 - 15, KJV. This being seduced by seducing spirits, starts with a wanton spirit. "Remember Lot's wife" Luke 17: 32, KJV. So we see a warning about wantoness even with the spiritual minded. The strong spiritually minded Christian can be seduced from a spiritual mindset as well. Adam and Eve were perfectly innocent when created and only knew what God was teaching them. But Satan, the prince of seducing spirits caused them to fall. And he used Eve's wantoness. Our minds have to be continually regenerated and renewed. Your mind feeds just like your body does. And the mind is grazing all day even at night in your sleep, filing the food you feed it during the day. Jesus said in Luke 11: 35, "Therefore take heed, that the light which is in you is not darkness", Luke 11: 35, NKJV.

The Regenerated Mind

What is being said when the scripture talks of the regenerated mind? First, it starts with the rebirth, being born again of the Holy Spirit as confirmed by John 3: 1 – 8, when Jesus was speaking to Nicodemus. Second, it is a beginning of the reprogramming of the mind due to the conviction and drawing of the Holy Spirit. Third, it is a steadfast commitment to perseverance in growing in the faith to produce the fruit of the Spirit. All plants produce fruit from the inside out, so the work of God in an individual is from the inside out or it isn't real.

The reprogramming of the mind begins through the revelation given by the Holy Spirit about our new life style, which is Christ Jesus, see Galatians 1: 11 12. This indoctrination of the things of the kingdom comes after the rebirth. The Holy Spirit will reveal the wisdom and life of Christ to our spirit, which contrasts the wisdom of this age. Jesus said that the Comforter the Holy Spirit whom He would send unto us would testify of Him, see John 15: 26, KJV. The Holy Spirit uses the scripture to reveal the life of Christ because Jesus is the word, see John 1: 1 & 14. So when He reveals the word He is testifying of Jesus Christ.

You are what you think and you gravitate toward what you desire. That is why Paul commanded us "And be renewed in the spirit of your mind." Ephesians 4: 23, KJV. The reason for this is God's wisdom and the wisdom of this age are opposites and hostile to one another. You also begin to attract whatever is your mindset. You actually create your personality, your environment, and your life through the thoughts and imaginations of the mind, programming your subconscious mind with habits of either the "Spirit or the Flesh".

Someone said that the greatest discovery man has ever made is, that man has the power of choice, to choose the kind of person he wants to be, and the things he wants to pursue in life. God ordained that we would choose a disposition of love, joy, peace, longsuffering, kindness, goodness, faith, gentleness, self-control, of personality, coupled with integrity and humility in character.

God is saying this in Genesis, "Then God said, "Let us make man in our image, after our likeness;....", Genesis 1: 26, KJV. The fruit of the Spirit is the likeness of God. God intended for all human kind to have His image so we can enjoy life by reaping good things into our life. Man forfeited that in the garden. Now, through Jesus Christ and through fellowship with Him and godly interaction with one another, that "Abundant Life " can be restored that Jesus promised in John 10: 10. The enemy came to rob you of good things, teaching and giving you an ill-natured disposition and filling you with self-destructive habits of personality and character that take away your well being.

And you hath he quickened who were dead in trespasses and sins; Wherein time past ye walked according to the course of this world, according to the prince of the power of the air, the spirit who now worketh in the children of disobedience.

Ephesians 2: 1 – 2, KJV.

A person is only made whole in Jesus Christ, is true. And the good thing is that He has come to do just that, John says, "He that comitteth sin is of the devil, for the devil has sinned from the beginning. For this purpose the Son of God was manifested that He might destroy the works of the Devil", 1

John 3: 8, KJV. And again in Ephesians 2: 10 says, "For we are His workmanship created in Christ Jesus for good works, which God prepared beforehand that we should walk in them". Ephesians 2: 10, KJV.

How does He destroy the works of the devil in our lives? By destroying the mindset and the wisdom we have learnt in our old life that comes from the world, the flesh, and the devil and replacing that wisdom with His wisdom and mindset. His mindset has to be pursued. In the past, we pursued the mindset of things that were not profitable now we pursue His mindset and become profitable to our growth in His image and our welfare. Paul said in verse two, "... the spirit who now works in the sons of disobedience", which is the unbeliever. First he said we are created in Christ Jesus - (made alive in, Chapter 2, verse 1). Second, we are the workmanship of Christ unto good works - *(a newness of life, chapter 2, and verse 10)*. Third, which God prepared, *(intended, again verse 10)* for human-kind before hand that we should walk in, see Genesis 1: 26 – *(Our image)*, the works of the Newness of Life, (Romans 6: 4)." See the NKJV. Jesus said to the devil in one place in Matthew:

But He turned and said to Peter, "Get behind Me Satan, you are an offense to Me, for thou savorest not the things (wisdom) that be of God, but that (that wisdom that) be of man.

Matthew 16: 23, KJV. (Emphasis mine*)*.

In another place He told James and John,

But He turned and rebuked them and said, "You do not know what manner of spirit *(wisdom)* you are of. For the Son

of Man is not come to destroy men's lives but to save them."
And they went to another village.

Luke 9: 55 – 56, KJV, *(Emphasis Mine)*.

A person truly going through the evolution of the new
creation in Christ Jesus and is changing and conforming to
His image, begins operating in another wisdom than that of
this world or of the spirit of this world. Their wisdom comes
from above. It is a gentler wisdom than this world and a just
wisdom coupled with compassion. Let us look at it from James's
perspective,

Who is wise and understanding among you? Let him show
by good conduct that his works are done in the meekness of
wisdom. But if you have bitter envy and self-seeking in your
hearts, do not boast and lie against the truth. This wisdom does
not descend from above, but is earthly, sensual, demonic. For
where envy and self-seeking exist, confusion and every evil
thing are there. But the wisdom that is from above is first pure,
then peaceable, gentle, willing to yield, full of mercy and good
fruits, without partiality and without hypocrisy. Now, the fruit
of righteousness is sown in peace by those who make peace.

James 3: 13 – 18, NKJV

As a person changes into His image, they become a person
of integrity, become personable, and full of goodness. This
is some of the wisdom spoken of in 1 Corinthians 2: 11 the
children of disobedience do not understand The wisdom of this
world teaches self preservation above all else. The wisdom that
is from above teaches a win – win value for all we deal with. If
our associates don't get a fair shake as well as us, we won't make
the deal. It is quick to listen and slow to speak.

When individuals begin to make progress and mature in God's wisdom, they are ready to accomplish great things with their life bringing glory to God and honor and peace to themselves. My son do not forget my law, but let your heart keep my commands, *(walk in my wisdom)* for length of days and long life and peace they will add to you." See Proverbs 3: 1 – 2, NKJV, *(Emphasis mine)*. The bible preached the law of attraction probably long before any name of the principle "Law of Attraction" became so prevalent as it is today. Growing saints mature in vitality, caring, and integrity because they choose that wisdom. Maturing Saints become more because they become goal oriented living a life of purpose:

Delight thyself also in the Lord; and he shall give you the desires of your heart.

Psalm 37: 4, KJV.

They labor to accomplish things that sow good into the lives of others and adding a wealth of good to their own welfare.

I am not talking about monetary wealth only, but making others rich by personal example that inspires others to be all they can be. They produce on purpose, one is personal growth spiritually and second secularly, having a vision of ourselves as to the core values we want to live by and be known for. You become a person with a dream and purpose in mind that has honest service to others as its' goal, not just seeking just your own welfare but the welfare of others also, that win – win in relations. Isn't that like God, they become even more fruitful through being purposely productive and giving through seeking God's honor and the welfare of society. Society begins with family, the church, the business, the career, and all they are involved with, see 1 Corinthians 10: 31 - 33. God's wisdom teaches us to lay down your life in serving the welfare of one another (See 1 John 3: 16 & 2 Corinthians 5: 14). Jesus taught being purposeful in Mark 9: 50 saying, "Have salt in youselves...

The life of godliness or god-likeness isn't meant to be understood as being a means for gain as it comes across in some circles, as Paul explains in 1 Timothy 6: 5. "But, Godliness *(obedience)* with contentment is great gain." 1 Timothy 6: 6, NIV, *(Emphasis Mine)*. The new life just serves for the satisfaction of it – it is it's own reward, "The Abundant Life", because we know the reward of inheritance is from the Lord, see Colossians 3: 23 – 24 and Ephesians 6: 7 – 9, KJV.

Let us realize that the "Abundant Life" does not mean a martyrdom life either. It means serving others for God's glory and the satisfaction it gives to be giving something back, expecting nothing in return. We do it because we hope it helps and it is the right thing to do. The wisdom of God teaches this as part of our new nature, it teaches a life style of a servant of all. A servant of all means seeking a win – win for every body. This we have received in Christ Jesus to God's glory, we are "New Creatures", 2 Corinthians 5: 17 and Galatians 6: 15. As we grow in Him there will less and less selfishness and more and more meekness.

Paul had purpose, hope, joy, and vitality radiating from his life in Christ. It is a new life making others rich, as His life's image develops in us. Paul was a fountain of living water that others drank from as he lived among them, walking in the wisdom of the Spirit, (See James 3: 13 – 18). Paul stated it this way, "as sorrowful, yet always rejoicing, as poor yet making many rich, as having nothing and yet possessing all things." 2 Corinthians 6: 10, KJV.

I had a grand mother that was always saintly and so joyful and full of sweetness, a person that pleasant to be around. She influenced everyone, especially her children and her grandchildren. Grandma Miller made everyone feel important and welcome, never complained or condemned, but just hoped for the best, "Leave it in Jesus Hands" was her mantra. She was protective of all of us when we were good or bad. She always made Christ the center of all her conversations, was a woman of integrity and service, as where her children. Mainly grandma Miller rubbed off on all her children and grand children in a good way because of the Christ in her. No one had anything bad to say of grandma. She had developed into the character and personality of Christ in her lifetime and inspired others through example and speech. She was being the light He had intended her to be to her generation. She made the lives of all she touched richer for knowing her. That is what God's wisdom being lived by us, works in and for us – we leave a life of significant good memories and service to others.

Seeing how we are all evolving creatures, this character and nature has to be developed. In Ecclesiastes it states,

Truly, this only I have found: that God made man upright, but they have sought out many schemes.

Ecclesiastes 7: 29, NKJV.

This means we started out with a clean slate. The experts say that at birth the neuron circuits in a baby's brain are only 17% connected. These connections are for the body organs to function properly and these connections are made while in the mothers' womb. The rest of the connections we make in life, creating habits and personality traits. These come from the thoughts and the actions inspired by our environment, along the wisdom and character traits we admire in others. This happens as we grow and develop as persons. Truly, we create our personality, our environment with the choices of our minds in the form of wisdom and goals we establish for our lives. You become what you admire and you attract more of what you are and become. James Allen put it this way in his book "As A Man Thinketh":

Thought in the mind hath made us. What we are by thought was wrought and built. If a man's mind hath evil thoughts, pain comes on him as comes the wheel the ox behind... if one endure in purity of thought, joy follow him as his own shadow – sure."

The bible says the same thing:

Or do you despise, the riches of His goodness, forbearance, and longsuffering, not knowing that the goodness of God leads you to repentance? But in accordance with your hardness and your impentinent heart you are treasuring up for yourself wrath in the day of wrath and revelation of the righteous judgment of God., who will render to each one according to his deeds, eternal life to those who by patient continuance in doing good seek for glory, honor, and immortality; but to those who are self seeking and do not obey the truth, but obey unrighteousness – indignation and wrath, tribulation and anguish, on every soul of man who does evil, of the Jew first and also of the Greek; but glory, honor, and peace to everyone who works what is good, to the Jew first and also the Greek. For there is no partiality with God.

Romans 2: 4 – 11, NKJV.

Living after the mind of the flesh causes a life of fear, anxiety, tribulation, (See Romans 2: 7 – 10). Living the life of God comes from a mind set on the temperamental traits and integrity of the Holy Spirit. This attracts health, honor, and peace. Peace in the bible means prosperity inwardly and outwardly.

The mind of the Spirit is full of loving imaginations for the welfare for others, and ourself. It is joyful because of a good conscious; grateful in spirit for God's grace in our lives; and at peace due the contentment that comes from knowing that God has you in His continual care. It does not allow negative complaining or grumbling to poison or dishearten. It is a life living in peace and in forbearance with others, yet not without a conscience toward Christ. It is patient with life and hardships, manifesting kindness, goodness, faithfulness, gentleness, and self control, in all relations and circumstances as defined in Galatians 5: 22. These are the excellent personality traits and habits in a person that will yield the peaceable fruit of righteousness. That peaceableness comes from a fellowship with God as well as the good conscious that gives. In addition, it comes from one that is committed to obeying the Spirit by fixing their mind on what the Spirit teaches. They pursue the discernment of the people skills taught in the scripture, applying them as core values for their life.

As said before, Paul prayed that God would grant that we would discern this new life. First, this life is learnt through knowledge, which comes from the scripture teaching of the Holy Spirit. Second, the successful application of this knowledge gives us better people skills iluminating his life and wisdom from our lives to others. We get wisdom by applying this discernment that this knowledge of Him gives in our everyday experiences maturing in loving people skills.

And this I pray, that your love may abound *(evolve)*, still more and more in knowledge and all discernment, that you may approve the things (behaviors) that are excellent *(honorable)*, that you may be sincere and without offense till the day of Christ, being filled with the fruits of righteousness which are by Jesus Christ to the glory and praise of God.

Philippians 1: 9 – 10, NKJV, *(Emphasis Mine)*.

The Spirit of God teaches these things, "For what man knows the things of a man except the spirit of the man which is in him? Even so no one knows the things of God except the Spirit of God," 1 Corinthians 2: 11, NKJV.

Paul says we are to begin right away walking in this new life. The best way to learn anything is to study and do it. Walk in what you know and skill and discernment will be given to you as you move forward through your experiences in life.

And not only that, but we also glory in tribulations, knowing that tribulation produces perseverance; and perseverance, character; and character, hope, Now hope does not disappoint, because the love of God has been poured out in out hearts by the Holy Spirit who was given to us.

Romans 5: 3 – 5, NKJV.

"Therefore we were buried with Him through baptism into death, that just as Christ was raised from the dead by the glory of the Father, even so we also should walk in newness of life." Romans 6: 4. As we walk in fellowship with the Spirit, pursuing the application of what he teaches about this new life, he gives more instruction into this new life. "Then Jesus spoke to them again saying, "I am the light of the world. He who follows Me *(My Spirit)* shall not walk in darkness, but have the light of life." John 8: 12, *(Emphasis Mine)*. Again it says, "Turn at my rebuke, surely I will pour My Spirit out on you. I will give you revelation knowledge and make My words known to you." See Proverbs 1: 23. A good teacher teaches you as you are able to bear it. Learning has stages. When you have learnt one skill, then another is taught till you become a master journeyman in people skills. That is what salesmen strive for and it has made some millionaires, it is the same with our walk with the Lord. Now for a little more understanding of our beginning.

CHAPTER II

"HOW DID WE GET THIS WAY?"

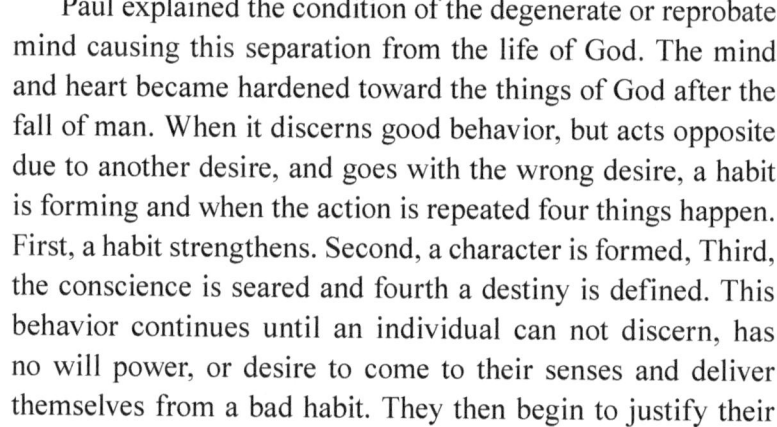

Paul explained the condition of the degenerate or reprobate mind causing this separation from the life of God. The mind and heart became hardened toward the things of God after the fall of man. When it discerns good behavior, but acts opposite due to another desire, and goes with the wrong desire, a habit is forming and when the action is repeated four things happen. First, a habit strengthens. Second, a character is formed, Third, the conscience is seared and fourth a destiny is defined. This behavior continues until an individual can not discern, has no will power, or desire to come to their senses and deliver themselves from a bad habit. They then begin to justify their behavior as in homosexuality, perverting the love of God and His word. When a person reaches this level he has confirmed his destiny. They cannot receive the teaching of the truth from the Spirit until they repent and are made alive, i.e. aware of the new life in Christ by the Spirit of God, Romans 1: 21 – 28 and:

And a servant of the Lord must not quarrel but be gentle to all, able to teach, patient, in humility correcting those who are in opposition, if God perhaps will grant them repentance, so that they may know the truth and that they may come to their senses and escape the snare of the devil, having been taken captive by him to do his will.

2 Timothy 2: 24 – 26, NKJV.

Those who are in opposition to the new life are taken captive by Satan to do his will. When God gives understanding or revelation to turn someone from error, that revelation of wisdom of the truth sets the person free from captivity of error, see John 8: 31 - 32. The carnal mind thinks that the things of God are foolishness, 1 Corinthians 2: 14. Largely due to the institutions of this world, Educational, Entertainment, and The Arts, also relationships. We learnt from these institutions and the relationships we have and they rub off on us, they feed us. Paul said this "Do not be deceived: "Evil company corrupts good habits", 1 Corinthians 15: 33,NKJV.

How many parents grieve over children that cannot seem to discern destructive behavior. The child cannot see that the wisdom of the parent is right and discern what is best for their welfare and happiness. God has the same grief, wanting the best for humanity, but we fight against and ignore His wisdom for our life and society. Listen! If our behavior causes harm to another, or ourselves, it is not God. Neither if our behavior defames His name. Let this be your guide, "The blessing of the Lord makes one rich, and adds no sorrow with it." Proverbs 10: 22. His wisdom promotes a win – win for His honor and yours. If it were God, you or no one else would suffer from it. HIV started with the homosexual community, how could that be from a loving God. That was caused by the evil schemes of man, due to the law of cause and effect. "This only have I found that God made man upright, but they have sought out many schemes." Ecclesiastes 7: 29, NKJV.

The imaginations of the mind create the lives we live; you are what you created in the mind through desire and the attitudes of the mind, you created your personality and environment. Your environment expresses it. That's why Paul commanded us "And be renewed in the spirit *(attitudes)* of your mind." Ephesians 4: 23, KJV, *(Emphasis Mine)*. Someone said that the greatest discovery man has ever made is that man has the power of choice, to choose the thoughts he thinks, the kind of character he wants, and the things he wants to pursue in life. You can have the abundant life God wants you to have, but we have to start thinking like Him, walking after His thoughts, and His desires. The old adage, "If you want to be a millionaire, you have to think like a millionaire". If you want to like be Godlike, you have to think like Him, is really a principle taught in the bible. You will know them by their fruits. Do men gather grapes from thornbushes or figs from thistles?" Matthew 7: 16, NKJV. So we have to watch who we learn from and we have to discipline our minds to right thinking and not let them entertain themselves with mental candy. Mental candy is the food of thornbushes. "Go from the presence of a foolish man, when you do not perceive in him the lips of knowledge." Proverbs 14: 7, NKJV.

Proverbs 4: 23 says it this way: "Keep your heart with all diligence, For out of it spring the issues of life." Alternatively speaking, you create the issues, joys and ills of life as James Allen asserted in a similar way in his book "As A Man Thinketh".

We have heard it said that people do not change, but with God, all things are possible. He gives the Christian an awareness of the new life by making us alive in Christ; this gives us a desire to change at the new birth. If all a person experiences is a New Year resolution and has not been reborn of the Spirit, he is not His and change will be minor if any. See John 3: 1 – 6.

The teaching of the Spirit is the revelation of the life of Jesus who is the image of God, Colossians 1:15 and Hebrews 1: 3. Paul goes into detail about this in Ephesians chapter four.

So I tell you this, and insist on it in the Lord, that you must no longer live as the Gentiles do in the futility of their thinking. They are darkened in their understanding and separated from the life of God because of the ignorance that is in them due to the hardening of their hearts. Having lost all sensitivity, they have given themselves over, to sensuality so as to indulge in every kind of impurity, with a continual lust for more. You however, did not come to know (the life of) Christ that way. Surely you heard of Him and were taught in Him in accordance with the truth that is in Jesus. You were taught with regard to your former life, to put off your old self *(life),* which is being corrupted by its deceitful desires; to be made new in the attitude of your minds and to put on the new self *(life),* created to be like God in true righteousness and holiness.

Ephesians 4: 17 – 24 NIV, *(Emphasis Mine)*.

Man refuses this life of God that God offers and in turn receives a life of self-destructing habits, see Romans 1: 28. Not every person goes to the same depth of reprobate discernment, a lot has to do with ones environment and associations. A large number seem to start out early in life learning unprofitable personality behavior and habits, largely from television and the entertainers they admire. This happens largely, if a child is not exposed to good teaching and mentors, but allowed to just feast on mental candy, which is one of the vices of this society. Paul shows how deep and degenerate a person can become, not that all believers go to those depths. A definition for lost is, not knowing where one is headed or going, just rolling with the punches aimlessly in life.

We have to reframe our thinking putting off the thoughts of the flesh nature, the old life and not feeding our minds with those examples in Hollywood that idolize the appeal of old life and the technological world of violent and "R" rated video games. We have to put on the thoughts of the Spirit, the new life to begin experiencing the life of God and the peace that comes with it. We will discuss this in the next chapter.

CHAPTER III

"THE LIFE OF GOD PRODUCES BETTER RESULTS"

But the hour is coming and now is, when the true worshippers will worship the Father in spirit and truth; for the Father is seeking such to worship Him, John 4: 24, NKJV.

Walking in the Spirit is walking from the inside out. God is seeking those who show their worship of Him by walking in this new life being created within, without hypocrisy, but sincerely. Sincerely means with full integrity of action and transparency, with no show. It is a life according to the character of Jesus Christ.

But you have not so learned Christ, if indeed you have heard Him and have been taught by Him, as the truth *(truth of life)* is in Jesus: that you put off, concerning your former conduct, the old man *(old life)* which grows corrupt *(self destructive)* according to the deceitful lust *(feelings and desires of man)* and be renewed in the spirit of your mind, and what you put on the new man *(new life)* which was created according to God, in true righteous and holiness. *(after the true character of Christ).*

Ephesians 4: 20 – 24, NKJV, *(Emphasis Mine)*.

Again Paul said it this way, "And those who are Christ have crucified the flesh with its passions and desires." Galatians 5: 24, NKJV. Paul said it this way in another place also, "For in Christ Jesus neither circumcision nor uncircumcision avails anything, but a new creation." Galatians 6: 15, NKJV. The new creation can not happen without the rebirth and your submission to the truth of God's word. Your effort begins with receiving the new birth and regeneration in the Holy Spirit, see Titus 3: 5, and the effort of disciplining the mind with focus on the new behavior taught in the scriptures. Jesus taught focus this way,

The lamp of the body is the eye *(the imagination)*. Therefore, when your eye is good *(wholesome/sound)*, your whole body also is full of light. But, when your eye is bad *(gross/degenerate)*, your whole body is full of darkness. Therefore, take heed that the light, which is in you, is not darkness. If then your whole body is full of light, having no part dark, the whole body will be full of light, as when the bright shining of a lamp gives you light. Emphasis mine.

Luke 11: 34 – 36, NKJV, *(Emphasis Mine)*. (See also 1 John 1: 5).

The eye of the body is the imagination. We want to make sure that our imagination is seeking and focussed on good things because as I said in similar way before, it is in the spirit of the mind that a man creates the issues of life. Wholesome things come into our life because we focus on wholesome things, due to the law of cause and effect, we gravitate to our strongest desires. Thoughts are things, just intangible to the naked eye. We gravitate to wholesome things or unwholesome things according to our thoughts and desires. God created the mind that way so we could create habits. We have 83% of our brain neurons left at birth, that have not made neuron connections. They are there for creating the habits we will have in life and they are meant to be godly habits after His image. "... For as he thinks in his heart, so is he." Proverbs 23: 7, NKJV.

Remember Ecclesiastes 7: 29, NKJV again, "Truly, this only I have found: that God made man upright, but they have sought out many schemes." Solomon is alluding to the connections in the brain whether he knew it or not. I understand that at birth 17% of neuron connections in the brain are made and are for running and regulating the body. The other 83% are for potentials in character, core values, personality, career skills, hobby skills, and inventions – the real us. We have so much potential that we will never use up all the connections in the brain. It is the most super organ known to man. That is why the bible has so much instruction concerning the mind, God knows what it can do, if used for His purposes, it creates good or it can create ill.

Those who would single-mindedly focus their thought life to think His thoughts and follow through on His core values, inherit honor, peace, and life. Look at Philippians 4: 8, Those who set their minds on those things and follow through in their spirit and the affairs of life are they who worship Him in Spirit. Walking after those things please Him see Romans 8: 6 - 8. "He who earnestly seeks good finds favor. But trouble will come to him who seeks evil", Proverbs 11: 27. You find favor with God and man. Proverbs 3 says it this way,

My son, do not forget my law *(My wisdom)*, But let your heart keep my commands *(My wisdom)*; For length of days and long life and peace they will add to you. Let not mercy and truth forsake you; Bind them around your neck, Write them on the tablet of your heart. And so find favor and high esteem in the sight of God and man.

Proverbs 3: 1 – 4, NKJV, (Emphasis Mine).

"But trouble *(self destruction)* will come to him who seeks evil *(who follows after evil wisdom)*." Proverbs 11: 27, NKJV, *(Emphasis Mine)*. See also Romans 2: 7 – 11 and Galatians 6: 7 - 10.

The Spirit will enable us to live out this newness of life we are to walk. The Holy Spirit illuminates the thought life with God's truth, which in turn transforms, when practiced. We transform or morph into the image of His life as we begin to increase in more knowledge about His life. By practicing we form new habits which are His habits. The truth of this life, the world cannot see because of the willful ignorance that is in them. It takes the drawing of the Holy Spirit (conviction of conscience) for a man to come to the acknowledgment of the truth about this life. Then it takes acceptance, repentance, effort, and submission to the self-discipline it takes to affect this change from our old habits to the new habits of this new life in Christ we have inherited.

For if you live according to the sinful nature you will die; but if by the Spirit you put to death the misdeeds of the body, you will live. Because those who are led by the Spirit *(by the wisdom of the Spirit)* of God, are the sons of God.

Romans 8: 13 – 14, NIV, *(Emphasis Mine)*

Solomon exhorts us this way, "Keep your heart with all diligence, for out of it spring the issues of life." Proverbs 4: 23, NKJV. As I stated earlier, for out of the thought life, the issues, circumstances and environment of life are created. By our thoughts, we create our circumstances, environment and character. These things are a reflection of our thoughts and of the life we have created from them. If you want to be more you have to become more by applying yourself more. You are were you are today because of the thoughts and choices you have made up until now. Your environment is truly a representation of your inner self. You can not change your destiny over night but you can change your direction overnight. Thus, eventually your destination by changing your thoughts, your philosophy of life, and the wisdom you use walk by in life.

To worship God in Truth is worshipping God in reality or acknowledging the reality of God as an ever present entity in your life. The scripture teaches to do this, we have to, "Trust in the Lord with all your heart. And lean not on your own understanding; in all your ways acknowledge Him and He shall make your paths straight." Proverbs 3: 5 – 6, NIV. Paul prayed for the Ephesians that Christ would live in their hearts by faith, see Ephesians 3: 17. Paul led by example in living this out in his own life.

I have been crucified with Christ, it is no longer I who live but *(but the life of),* Christ lives in me and the life which I now live in the flesh I live by faith in the Son of God who loved me and gave Himself for me," *(Emphasis Mine).*

Galatians 2: 20, NKJV.

What Solomon and Paul are saying is that as we acknowledge what God has done for us in Christ Jesus and by faith, we apply His ways, making them our way of life. Walking in faith of His transforming and care and keeping is explained by Peter this way, "Wherefore let them that suffer according to the will of God, commit of their souls to Him in well doing, as unto a faithful Creator," 1 Peter 4: 19, KJV. For, "He that sayeth he abides in Him ought himself also to walk even as He walked." 1 John 2: 6, KJV. Let us look at this walk of faith in another light.

When God acknowledged King Saul in 1 Samuel 10: 6 – 7, He made an awesome promise to Saul.

Then the Spirit of the Lord will come upon you, and you will prophesy with them and be turned into another man, let it be, when these signs come to you, that you do as the occasion demands, for God is with you.

1 Samuel 10: 6 – 7, NKJV.

Paul said, "Therefore if anyone is in Christ, he is a new creation; old things have passed away, behold all things have become new. Now all things are of God...." 2 Corinthians 5: 17 –18. When the Holy Spirit comes into our life, He gives us an awareness or witness inside that God is with us by the very essence of His presence in us. We realize everything matters to God and everything is of God, received from God and is in His control. We have trouble believing it when things seem to be falling apart or alarm us. However Saul is being told to walk by faith and handle the occasions of life and God would be with him to keep him to direct his steps and make them straight.

When He said in Genesis, "Let us, make man in Our image," He was talking of a development process as in child development, go back and look at Ecclesiastes 7: 29.

We become the average of the inner circle in our lives. If you don't like the results your getting, something has to change and it starts with your thoughts, choices, and friends you hang with. Are they inventors of evil things and idolize the things of the world. God was going to be Adam and Eve's mentor but when they fell, He gave that position up to Adam and Eve to learn from their own nature and Satan's scheming against them. They followed the wisdom of self-preservation and Satan. It was not until the time of Enos that the bible mentions that men began to call upon the Lord, Genesis 4: 26. They learnt their wisdom from their fallen nature – they had no fellowship with the Spirit of God. You become what or who you are influenced by, (See Ecclesiastes 7: 29).

After we have become aware, that all things are from God, even Satan, and begin to have fellowship with Him, He allows us chances to make the right choices to develop us into His image and to learn of Him. We learnt about Satan and self preservation, now we learn about serving and the Father that is revealed in the person of Jesus Christ. He did this with Saul who failed the test and proved unfaithful and became reprobate to the dealings of God due to being willful and presumptuous. The dealings of God are mentioned in Hebrews 12: 5 – 13, that we will get into later.

He uses our choices letting us reap what we sow and uses what we reap for our good to lead us to repentance if wrong or growth if right choices were made. The pressures of life are for our development and growth of mind. God doesn't want His children to be small minded, He wants them serve others and dream big in life. By the pressures in life, our development takes place, leading to repentance of the habits that give us unwanted results. Our lives begin to change for the better because we are becoming more. By becoming more we become more valuable to ourself and to those associated with us. Through these situations of life the process of sanctification works, conforming us to His image as we make the right choices conforming to His ways taught in His word. This causes that which is lame about us to become healed (See Hebrews 12: 11 – 13). We are all lame somewhere, developing into the person God wants us to be, is a journey and a destination to pursue in this life. Paul said in 1 Corinthians 15: 31, KJV, "... I die daily." We are being regenerated by the washing and regeneration of the Spirit. The washing away of the wisdom and habits of the old life and regenerating us by developing in us the wisdom and habits of the new life, See Titus 3: 5, and Ephesians 5: 26.

Practicing the habits of God's life, the new life, causes us to come out of the circumstances we reaped on ourselves. These destructive bad habits, we learnt from the Spirit of the air, that works in the children of disobedience as stated in Ephesians 2: 2, bring unwanted circumstances on us. However, the good habits we learn from the Holy Spirit of Christ, who teaches the life of God (See 1 Corinthians 2: 11 - 14), begins to bring good things into our life. The results are the inner man and his outward circumstances begin to improve due to these new habits. These new habits allow us to start reaping better relationships and consequences until our life becomes whole again. Then is the old adage "Jesus made me whole" is revealed. "And you shall know the truth and the truth will set you free", if you walk in it, See John 8: 32. Jesus is saying it will make the lame in behavior whole, setting you free from your self-destructive attitudes and habits.

When we begin to walk in the self destructive habits of the flesh, we become self destructive. This is because the mindset of the flesh is hostile to your own welfare as well as to God who wants our best. He came to give you life and that life more abundant. The carnal mind teaches us to seek after pleasure, the road less traveled, and self preservation, etc. This type of life style leads to an aimless life of greed that only produces an existence were someone always suffers or is neglected for our preservation and pleasure.

Walking after the thoughts of the Spirit, walking after His ways and His purposes for our life, leads to a life of service to others and well being for us. We will find ourselves taking taking the "Higher Road". God's way is the higher road. Isaiah asserts it:

For my thoughts are not your thoughts, neither are your ways my ways declares the Lord. As the heavens are higher than the earth, so are my ways higher than your ways and my thoughts than your thoughts.

Isaiah 55: 8 – 9, NIV.

In verse 7 of the same chapter, God tells us we have gone astray from His plan for us in that, He exhorts us to change the way we think and behave. "Let the wicked forsake his way, and the evil man his thoughts. Let him turn to the Lord.... Isaiah 55: 7, NIV. How do we turn?" We turn to thinking like Him - on His thoughts, His desires, and His ways. We exchange the mindset of the world, the flesh, and the devil for the mindset of the Spirit. When thought and action become one, habits are being formed and the if we have developed bad habits, the great thing about it is that we can learn new habits. Experience tells us it can be accomplished by practice over a period of six to eight weeks. And experts also say that as new habits can be stopped and that they weaken and can also suffer atrophy just like when we stop exercising and muscles atrophy. The mind can suffer atrophy also. But there will always be a struggle to learn new habits, and because of the struggle people like to take the road of least resistance and make excuses for the way they are. "I was made like this." But not by God, we make ourselves with the tools He gave us. The tools are thought and imagination, and thoughts and imaginations can be changed!

"If then you were raised with Christ, seek those things which are above, where Christ is sitting at the right hand of God. Set your mind on things above, not on things on the earth." Colossians 3: 1 – 2, NKJV. And again Paul asserts: "Finally brethern, whatever things are true, whatever things are noble, whatever things are just, whatever things are of good report, if there is any virtue, and if there is anything praiseworthy

– meditate on these things." Philippians 4: 8, NKJV. As we do this He works in us to will and do of His good pleasure, see Philippians 2: 13. His good pleasure is the habitual habits of doing things that are of excellent and honorable in conduct, full of His desires. His desires are loving concern for us, thus ours should be for the welfare of our neighbor, not just our own. Seeking a win - win for each other in all our dealings with our neighbor, not trying to take advantage of them.

Hebrews 12: 5 – 13 tells us that God allows everything in our life with a purpose, for our training in holiness. If we humble ourselves in faith acknowledging His hand at work in us it will effect change. We are to be evolving, allowing ourselves to be trained by life's circumstances and not defeated by them, The we become skilled and established in excellent, Godlike, and honorable habits.

And you have forgotten the exhortation which speaks to you as to sons: 'My son, do not despise the chastening of the Lord, nor be discouraged when you are rebuked by Him; For whom the Lord loves He chastens, and scourges every son He receives.' If you endure chastening, God deals with you, as with sons, for what son is there whom a father does not chasten? But if you are without chastening, of which all have become partakers, then you are illegitimate and not sons. Furthermore, we have had human fathers who corrected us, and we paid them respect. Shall we not much more readily be in subjection to the Father of spirits and live? For they indeed for a few days chastened us as seemed best to them, but He for our profit, that we may be partakers of His holiness. Now no chastening seems to be joyful for the present, but painful; nevertheless, afterward it yields the peaceable fruit of righteousness to those who have been trained by it. Therefore strengthen the hands which hang down, and the feeble knees and make straight paths for your feet, so that what is lame may not be dislocated, but rather be healed.

Hebrews 12: 5 – 13, NKJV.

Also, "And we know that all things work together for good to those who love God, to those who are the called according to His purpose." Romans 8: 28, NKJV. God has promised to make everything work for our good, if we submit to Him in every situation. This life is a hassle, it takes faith in God or you will be overwhelmed from trying to live it in your own strength. This is what God was exhorting Saul to understand in 1 Samuel 10: 6 - 7. This Fatherly training is to give us practice in developing the excellent behavioral habits of His life, and character. Then our life and character evolve in healing that which is lame in our life and character as we walk in it. All the while His promise to us is, "... for God is with you." 1 Sam 10: 6 –7, stated earlier.

Jesus put it this way in Matthew:

Come unto Me, all you who labor and are heavy laden, and I will give you rest. Take My yoke upon you, and learn from Me, for I am gentle and lowly in heart, and you will find rest for your souls. For My yoke is easy and My burden is light.

Matthew 11: 28 – 30, NKJV.

Lets us go on to know the Lord and grow in Him and we will find rest from a self-destructive life, as He perfects, matures, and establishes us in the new life by His working in us, see Ephesians 3: 20. It will produce an abundant life that glorifies Him and brings glory, honor and peace to us – expect it as David did. "Surely goodness and mercy will follow me all the days of my life, and I will dwell in the house of the Lord forever. Psalm 23: 6, NKJV.

Peter exhorted us to this end.

You therefore, beloved, since you know this beforehand, beware lest you also fall from your own steadfastness, being led away with the error of the wicked; but grow in the grace and knowledge of our Lord and Savior Jesus Christ. To Him be the glory both now and forever. Amen.

2 Peter 3: 17 – 18, NKJV.

It takes an exerted effort, it doesn't come automatically. As you begin to grow in the "Grace and the Knowledge of God" - you become fountains of living waters in this world. It is said that the church has the answers for the world. They that are being changed by the Spirit of God do understand the answer – Rest in Him as He makes you fountains of living waters.

CHAPTER IV

"BECOMING FOUNTAINS OF LIVING WATER"

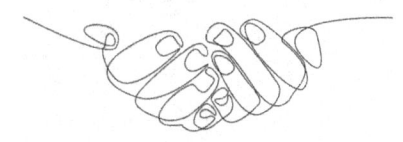

Jesus told the woman at the well:

Jesus answered and said to her, "Whoever drinks of this water will thirst again, but whoever drinks of the water that I shall give him will never thirst. But the water that I shall give him will become in him a fountain of water springing up into everlasting life.

John 4: 13 – 14, NKJV.

The living waters Jesus is talking about is the wisdom gained by the fellowship of the Holy Spirit dwelling in the inner man. The recipient of this fellowship is learning to engraft His word into their heart, becoming written epistles know and read of all men, see 2 Corinthians 3: 3. As we let God's wisdom dwell in us in all spiritual wisdom and understanding, it becomes a fountain of living waters in us, working in us His works, Philippians 2: 13. Applying it to all our ways by faith, we become fountains of living waters to others. Jesus was saying we would be refreshed ourselves by the fellowship of the Holy Spirit and in turn refresh the lives of others just as He did, John 4: 10 – 14, & 14: 12. Billy

Graham comes to mind as one that has developed into God's virtuous and holy nature. He has become a fountain of these living waters to those he meets, a fountain of living wisdom. This fountain of wisdom wells up in us to mature character which ensures eternal life.

Paul said it this way:

Now thanks be to God who always leads us in triumph in Christ, and through us diffuses the fragrance of His knowledge in every place. For we are to God the fragrance of Christ among those who are being saved and among those who are perishing. To the one, we are the aroma of death leading to death, and to the other the aroma of life leading to life. And who is sufficient for these things.

2 Corinthians 2: 14 – 16, NKJV.

The wisdom that God gives us to walk in is always honest, clean and positive. James describes this wisdom as a gift of God this way, "Do not be deceived, my beloved brethren. Every good gift and perfect gift is from above and comes down from the Father of lights, with whom there is no variation or shadow of turning." James 1: 16 – 17, NKJV. *(Wisdom is a perfect gift, it comes from God. Satan does not give good wisdom.)* Of His own will He brought us forth by the word of truth, that we might be a kind of first fruits of His creatures. So then, my beloved brethren let every man be swift to hear, slow to speak, slow to wrath; for the wrath of man does not produce the righteousness of God. Therefore lay aside all filthiness and overflow of wickedness, and receive with meekness the implanted word, which is able to save your souls."

James 1: 16 – 21, NKJV, *(Emphasis Mine)*.

Notice James says don't be deceived by the wisdom of this world, the wisdom of the flesh, the world, and the Devil by assuming it is of God, he says it in verse 13 – 14, NKJV:

Let no one say when he is tempted, "I am tempted by God"; for God cannot be tempted by evil, nor does He Himself tempt anyone. But each one is tempted when he is drawn away by his own desires and enticed.

God's good gifts include nothing evil being tempted by Him so where does it come from? The Prince of seduction, the Devil's wisdom. Good wisdom is revealed by the Spirit of God as I said earlier, Paul asserts:

But we speak the wisdom of God in a mystery, the hidden wisdom which God ordained before the ages for our glory,..... But God has revealed them to us through His Spirit. For the Spirit searches all things, yes the deep things of God. For what man knows the things of a man except the spirit of the man, which is in him? Even so, no one knows the things *(wisdom)* of God except the Spirit of God.... But the natural man does not receive the things *(wisdom)* of the Spirit of God, for they are foolishness to him; nor can he know them, because they are spiritually discerned."
1 Corinthians 2: 7 – 14, NKJV, *(Emphasis Mine)*.

The bible distinguishes between the wisdom that is of the world and the wisdom that is of God in James 3: 13 – 17, (Emphasis Mine),

Who is wise and understanding among you? Let him show by good conduct that his works are done in the meekness of wisdom. But if you have bitter envy and self-seeking in your hearts, do not boast and lie against the truth. This wisdom does not descend from above, but is earthly, sensual, demonic (get that, temptation to do evil is demonic wisdom). For where envy and self-seeking exist, confusion and every evil thing are there. But, the wisdom that is from above *(from God)* is first pure, then peaceable, gentle, willing to yield, full of mercy, and good fruits, without partiality and without hypocrisy. Now the fruit of righteousness is sown in peace by those who make peace.

James 3: 13 – 17, NKJV, *(Emphasis Mine)*.

God does not want us to learn the wisdom of this world as Paul further states in Romans, "... but I want you to be wise in what is good, and simple *(innocent)* concerning evil", Romans 16: 19, NKJV, *(Emphasis Mine)*. Jesus said it first in Matthew. "Behold, I send you out as sheep in the midst of wolves. Therefore, be wise as serpents and harmless as doves", Matthew 10: 16, NKJV. Paraphrased be wise in what is good discernment as serpents and innocent concerning evil as doves.

"But we all, with unveiled face, beholding as in a mirror the glory *(wisdom)* of the Lord, are being transformed into the same image from glory to glory, just as by the Spirit of the Lord." 2 Corinthians 3: 18, *(Emphasis Mine)*. We are evolving into the image of Christ by living and practicing in deed the wisdom taught by the Holy Spirit and He only teaches the wisdom of God, which is Christ. "... But you have not so learned Christ, if indeed you have heard Him and have been taught by Him, as the truth is in Jesus", Ephesians 4: 17 – 21, NKJV. "Then Jesus said to those Jews who believed Him, "If you abide in My word, you are My disciples indeed, and you shall know the truth, and the truth will set you free." John 8: 31 – 32, NKJV.

The Holy Spirit testifies to us of the wisdom of God's truth in the person of Jesus Christ, which is the image *(character and wisdom)* of Christ. God purposes in this is that we take on the image of Christ through the mentorship of the Holy Spirit. The Holy Spirit want make us change it is our choice. If we want His fellowship we will. However, we are the engineers of our character according to the wisdom we choose to submit to. We create - engineer ourselves with the thoughts, imagination, and philosophy of life we chose to live by. As we chose to submit to His wisdom, His character begins to evolve and starts redefining our life into that of fruitful Saints. We are called to walk worthy of our vocation in Christ in Ephesians 4: 1 in the King James Version. Our vocation or calling is that of Saints. Our lives will manifest more of His power working in us through the choices we begin to make in sync with His wisdom and character. All saints have this work going on in them. As we stay filled with the inspiration of the Holy Spirit, letting the word He reveals to us abide, continue in us in all spiritual wisdom and understanding, as in Colossians 3: 16, He changes us from glory to glory, destroying the wisdom and habits of Satan in our hearts and minds. "... For this purpose the Son of God was manifested, that He might destroy the works of Satan." 1 John 3: 8, NKJV. Satan works through his wisdom we have been inspired by in the past, or the Holy Spirit works in us through the wisdom of God that He teaches and inspires. It is our choice concerning whose wisdom we will follow. You become the child of whose wisdom you follow either Devil or children of God. Jesus addressed the Jews further like this:

You do the deeds of your father. Then they said to Him, "We were not born of fornication; we have one Father God." Jesus said to them, "If God were your Father, you would love Me, for I proceeded forth and came from God; nor have I come of Myself, but He sent Me. Why do you not understand My speech? Because you are not able to listen to My word, (See 1

Corinthians 2: 7 – 14). You are of your father the devil, and the desires of your father you want to do. He was a murderer from the beginning, and does not stand in the truth, because there is no truth in him. When he speaks a lie, he speaks from his own resources, for he is a lair and the father of it.

John 8: 41 – 44, NKJV.

The change that the Holy Spirit produces in us is the evidence of His power and His teaching working in us, see 1 Corinthians 4: 19 – 20. Paul says he was made an Apostle according to the effective working of His power at work in him according to Ephesians 3:7. Paul asserted it was God working in Him to do the ministry and teach God's wisdom in Colossians:

Him we preach, warning every man and teaching every man in all wisdom, that we may present every man perfect in Christ Jesus. To this end, I also labor, striving according to His working which works in me mightily.

Colossians 1: 28 – 29, NKJV.

As His power and influence works in us through the wisdom taught and power of Holy Spirit, we begin to mature in character to a place where God can begin to use us as lights. Then we become prepared and meet for every good work as spoken of in 2 Timothy 2: 19 - 21. Then he can use us for the furtherance of the gospel because our word and example line up.

Nevertheless, the solid foundation of God stands, having this seal: "The Lord knows those who are His," and, "Let everyone who names the name of Christ depart from iniquity." But in a great house there are not only vessels of gold and silver, but also of wood and clay, some for honor and some for dishonor.

Therefore if anyone cleanses himself from the latter, he will be a vessel for honor, sanctified and useful for the Master, prepared for every good work.

2 Timothy 2: 19 – 21, NKJV.

Paul speaks of those who claim to have life changing power, but are just puffed up with religious notions and feelings but cannot get their life in order.

But I will come to you shortly, if the Lord wills, and I will know, not the word of those who are puffed up, but the power. For the kingdom of God is not in word but in power,"

1 Corinthians 4: 19 – 20.

If there isn't a manifested change in life their faith and religion are vain. If His life is evolving in us, it is redefining our lives and our life's work. His wisdom is intertwined in all that we say and do. Jesus said, "... The kingdom of God does not come with observation; nor will they say, 'See here!' Or 'See there!' For indeed, the kingdom of God is within you." Luke 17: 20 – 21, NKJV. The work of God is happening and evident in you by the changes taking place. Everything in nature grows all it can, to its' capacity. Saints should be zealous to grow as much as than can like Christ, see 1 Timothy 4: 15 - 16.

Meditate upon these things; give thyself wholly to them; that thy profiting may appear to all. Take heed unto thyself, and unto the doctrine; continue in them; for in doing this thou shalt both save thyself, and them that hear thee. 2 Timothy 4: 15 – 16, KJV.

As we study this life, God's wisdom reveals His principles for living as it applies for conducting our affairs. His wisdom applies to our families, social activity, and our work ethic. It defines the life style He ordained for us to live as His children and ambassadors in this world for Him, see 2 Corinthians 5: 20. If the life of God is residing in you, it is revealed in word, in conduct, in love, in spirit, in faith and in purity, (See 1 Timothy 4: 12).

The Holy Spirit also teaches resolve, focus, and courage for a life of purpose, Jesus said, "... Have salt *(purpose)* in your yourselves and have peace one with another." Mark 9: 50, KJV, *(Emphasis Mine)*. We can see now that our lives become a fragrance of Christ as these fountains of living waters or fountain of living wisdom begin to flow from our inner being. This working identifies us as disciples of Jesus Christ with the Holy Spirit dwelling within. Then our lives begin to have influence, and who is sufficient for these things to be made ready to be fellow laborers with God. Paul asserts this in 2 Corinthians 2: 16 and 1 Corinthians 3: 8 – 10, NKJV. Holy Spirit work on!

Even a skilled tradesman or executive that has learnt their trade, those that are in high demand, study to become so. They go through a learning process and we to have to go through a learning process to change our personality and character as well. Good character is in high demand as well as good skill in careers; and that is what the Holy Spirit teaches and advocates to us to gain our willingness to let Him work it in us. We can do this knowing that in alarming situations God is our keeper. "....Working in you both to will and do of His good purpose. Philippians 2: 13, NKJV (See also Philippians 1:6).

A Call To Discernment

Paul addressed Timothy and Titus about false workers that have no power in their life also. "... having a form of godliness, but denying its' power. And, from such people turn away.... always learning and never able to come to the knowledge of the truth." 2 Timothy 3: 1 –7, NKJV. He reaffirms it to Titus, "They profess to know God, but in works *(Character)* they deny Him, being abominable, disobedient, and disqualified for every good work." Titus 1: 16, NKJV, *(Emphasis Mine)*. Character is built one work or act at a time, but it only takes one act to destroy it. We can disqualify ourself by just one act of indiscretion, see Hebrews 12: 16.

Everything moves these workers when they are out of their comfort zone or tried by temptation. They are still walking after their old nature. This new life receives power from the Holy Spirit to change a person over from the old life to the new life. Paul prayed this way for the Ephesians, "That he would grant you, according to the riches of his glory, to be strengthened with might by his Spirit in the inner man." Ephesians 3: 16, KJV. You have power to change but, unless you are zealous to seek it, continue in the teaching of Holy Spirit, and incorporate the doctrine of Christ into your heart; it will not take place. It is said in one place, "Buy the truth, and sell it not, also wisdom and instruction and understanding." Proverbs 23: 23, KJV. How do you sell it? Stop using it! If you stop learning, you start losing ground. "The backslider in heart shall be filled with his own ways *(old ways)*, but a good man will be satisfied from himself", Proverbs 14: 14, KJV *(Emphasis Mine)*. You will eat the fruit of your works reaping what you deserve. Do realize God did not design life to give you your needs? No! He designed life to give you what you deserve. You reap what you sow. "Be not deceived God is not mocked; for whatsoever a man soweth, that shall he also reap." Galatians 6: 7, KJV."

It is the same in seeking a trade or college degree, if you do not apply yourself to learn with the purpose of mastering a skill; you will always drift and achieve little and work for someone else. Working for someone else is not all-bad if it gets you where you want to be in life. You have to become good at what you do to make any real living. Learn a skill and sell it not – if you stop using it you will get rusty - it is the same as selling it – you sell it to neglect! So we do not want to neglect the truth.

My point is godly wisdom is taught by the Holy Spirit and applied by its' true seekers. If you are not seeking to learn godliness and character - you are not learning about them or growing in the knowledge of God and His character. However, you may be growing religiously indifferent and cynical. Again it is the same with gaining a trade, skill or talent; you have to pay the price, and the price is commitment. When you hear your favorite musician and say I wish I could play like that, they spent hours practicing and learning – they paid the price of commitment. To learn from the Holy Spirit you have to pay the price of spending time in God's word, praying, and obeying. This way you let the Comforter be your tutor and mentor, to grow you in the virtues of Christ. This is the only way to grow in the grace and knowledge of Him. Paul says it this way:

But reject profane and old wives' fables, and exercise yourself toward godliness. For bodily exercise profits a little, but godliness is profitable for all things, having promise of the life that now is and of that which is to come.

1 Timothy 4: 7 –8, NKJV.

The promise that now is, is the abundant life Jesus promised us in John 10: 10.

Jesus said, "Blessed are those who mourn, for they shall be comforted." Matthew 5: 4. Those who mourn are they that have a broken and contrite spirit due to seeking for fellowship, forgiveness and for wholeness in character and life. God promises, if we are mourning for the right thing comfort will come. That comfort is the answer for that which we are mourning for from Him and it aligns itself with God's wisdom in attaining wholeness of the person. It is a good thing to mourn for more fellowship with Him and more knowledge of Him to gain more wisdom in His word. Another meaning for mourning is to grieve for lack of or loss of something. In this case, we have a lack of understanding of Him and His ways. For He said "Blessed are they that hunger and thirst for righteousness, they shall be filled." Matthew 5: 6. He said, "If ye then, being evil, know how to give good gifts unto your children, how much more shall your Father which is in heaven give good things to them that ask him." Matthew 7: 11, KJV.

Wisdom is a good thing to ask of God. Solomon asked for wisdom and it pleased God so much that He promised him more riches and honor than anyone before him or after him because he asked for wisdom and not for things. (See 1 Kings 3: 9 – 14). James says, "If any of you lacks wisdom, let him ask of God, that giveth to all men liberally, and upbraideth not, and it shall be given him." James 1: 5, KJV.

However, the workers without power are always concerned with creature comforts more than asking for the things that please God. Jesus described them this way:

Watch out for false prophets. They come to you in sheep's clothing, but inwardly they are ferocious wolves. By their fruits *(their works in their affairs in life)*, you will recognize them. Do men pick grapes from thornbushes or figs from thistles? Likewise, every good tree bears good fruit, but a bad tree bears bad fruit. A good tree cannot bear bad fruit, and a bad tree cannot bear good fruit. Every tree that does not bear good fruit *(conduct)* is cut down and thrown into the fire. Thus by their fruit *(works / conduct)* you will recognize them.

Matthew 7: 15 – 21, NIV, *(Emphasis Mine)*.

Peter addressed them like this,

But these, like natural brute beasts made to be caught and destroyed, speak evil *(negative)* of the things they do not understand, and will utterly perish in their own corruption, and will receive the wages of unrighteousness, as those who count it pleasure to carouse in the daytime. They are spots and blemishes, carousing in their own deceptions while they feast with you, having eyes full of adultery and that cannot cease from sin, enticing unstable souls. They have a heart trained in covetous practices, and are accursed children. They have forsaken the right way and gone astray, following the way of Balaam the son of Beor, who loved the wages of unrighteousness; but was rebuked for his iniquity; a dumb donkey speaking with a man's voice restrained the madness of the prophet. These are wells without water; clouds carried by a tempest, for whom is reserved the blackness of darkness forever. For when they speak great swelling words of emptiness, they allure through the lusts of the flesh, through lewdness, the ones who have actually escaped from those who live in error. While they promise them liberty, they themselves are slaves of corruption; for by whom a person is overcome, by him also he is brought into bondage. For, after they have escaped the pollution's of the world through the knowledge *(and gained wisdom)* of the Lord and Savior Jesus Christ, they are again entangled in them and overcome, the latter end is worse for them than the beginning."

2 Peter 2: 12 – 20, NKJV, *(Emphasis Mine)*.

Another affirmation of these workers is in Jude:

But these speak evil of whatever they do not know; and whatever they know naturally, like brute beasts, in these things they corrupt themselves. Woe to them! For they have gone in the way of Cain, have run greedily in the error of Balaam for profit, and perished in the rebellion of Korah. These are spots in your love feasts, while they feast with you without fear, serving only themselves. These are clouds without water, carried about by the winds; late autumn trees without fruit, and twice dead, pulled up by the roots; raging waves of the sea, foaming up their own shame; wandering stars for whom is reserved the blackness of darkness forever. Now Enoch, the seventh from Adam, prophesied about these men also, saying, Behold, the Lord comes with ten thousands of His saints, to execute judgment on all to convict all who are ungodly among them of all their ungodly deeds which they have committed in an ungodly way, and of all the harsh things which ungodly sinners have spoken against Him." These are grumblers, complainers, walking according to their own lusts; and they mouth great swelling words, flattering people to gain advantage. But you, beloved, remember the words which were spoken before by the apostles of our Lord Jesus Christ: how they told you that there would be mockers, in the last time who would walk according to their own ungodly lusts. These are sensual persons, who cause divisions, not having the Spirit.

Jude 10 – 19, NKJV.

Jude gives us the remedy, "But you beloved, building yourselves up on your most holy faith, *(in the wisdom of the faith)*, praying in the Holy Spirit, keep yourselves in the love of God, looking for the mercy of our Lord Jesus Christ unto eternal life." *(Emphasis Mine)*,

Jude 20 –21, NKJV.

In addition, Paul exhorts us to pursue goodness, righteous, and truth, see Ephesians 5: 8 – 9 & 2 Timothy 2: & 22, (Emphasis Mine).

The more time spent with someone, the more you begin to take on some of their traits and mannerisms. The more time spent in the word and with the Holy Spirit the more fruits *(attitude and godliness)* of the Spirit you begin to manifest. You begin to have an attractive personality, "... love, joy, peace, longsuffering, kindness, goodness, faithfulness, gentleness, self-control. Against such is no law." Galatians 5: 22. I think these traits make a person attractive, don't you! We tend to be self-conscience, and concerned with our outward appearance, and do not think of what our personalities look like. However God says:

Do not let your adornment be merely outward – arranging the hair, wearing gold, or putting on fine apparel – rather let it the hidden person of the heart, with the incorruptible beauty of a gentle and quiet spirit, which is very precious in the sight of God.

1 Peter 3: 3 –4, NKJV.

God's power is manifested by your changed personality and character, the stripping away of the old man the bible calls him, and clothing us with the image of Christ, your new personality - the new man the bible calls him (See Ephesians 4:22 – 24). Our personalities and principles is the clothing of the Spirit, the inner man addressed in 1 Peter 3: 3- 4. What fashion wear our Spirit is wearing is noticeable.

You begin wearing the right Spiritual clothing - you begin to become bondservants of Christ and are His workmanship unto good works through the transformation of the Spirit. You become a masterpiece of God. What Satan, the world, and the flesh has worked in you, dressing your Spirit in the habits of the flesh, Christ has come to destroy that clothing of the spirit, see 1 John 3: 8 again. The dress clothes of the spirit are now after the image of him that gives life. He works in your life your mind and personality, giving you a new set of clothing. John put it this way; "The one who practices sin is of the devil; for the devil has sinned from the beginning. The Son of God appeared for this purpose, to destroy the works (clothing given us) of the devil." 1 John 3: 8 – 9, NASB.

As the Spirit begins to destroy the behavior of Satan in an individual, He replaces them with His behavior and good works, the character traits taught by the Spirit of Christ. "And you He hath quickened, who were dead in trespasses and sins, Wherein in time past ye walked according to the course of this world, according to the prince of the power of the air, the spirit that now worketh in the children of disobedience." Ephesians 2: 1 – 2, KJV. Satan works his desires in the unbeliever and hypocrite without them knowing it because of the ignorance in them concerning the life of God. In the case of hypocrite, his complacency, indifference, and luke warmness is their downfall. Verse 10 states, "For we are His workmanship created in Christ Jesus for good works *(conduct)*, which God prepared beforehand that we should walk in them," Ephesians 2: 10, *(Emphasis Mine)*. When the Holy Spirit makes us alive in Christ, He begins a work of teaching good conduct and works that are good – His character traits and principles in us.

Let us look at a scripture example of the sons of disobedience. Jesus was in an intense discussion with the Pharisees once and

He in reality calls them son of disobedience telling them that they were sons of the devil.

> You are of your Father the devil, and the desires of your father you want to do. He was a murderer from the beginning, and does not stand in the truth, because there is no truth in him. When he speaks a lie, he speaks from his own resources *(wisdom)*, for he is a lair and the father of it. But because I tell you the truth, you do not believe Me. Which of you convicts Me of sin? And, if I tell the truth, why do you not believe Me? He who is of God hears God's words: therefore you do not hear, because you are not of God.

John 8: 44 – 47, NKJV, *(Emphasis Mine)*.

Those that have become God's workmanship, he says this to them, "Then Jesus said to those Jews who believed him, "If you hold to my teaching; you are really my disciples *(workmanship)*. Then you will know the truth and the truth will set you free." John 8: 31 –32, NIV, *(Emphasis Mine)*.

God is continually at work in you and has promised not to allow you to be tempted above what you are able. Paul said, "Being confident of this very thing, that he which hath begun a good work in you will perform until the day of Jesus Christ." Philippians 1: 6, KJV. However, you have to abide in this work. Let me show you what I mean.

> Wherefore, my beloved, as ye have always, obeyed, not as in my presence only, but not much more in my absence, work out your own salvation with fear and trembling. For it is God which worketh in you to both to will and to do of his good pleasure.

Philippians 2: 12 – 13, KJV

You have to except life's circumstances as God's hands on training to establish you in His behavior. You have to follow His wisdom to be set free from the wisdom of the enemy of your souls. May you seek to let Jesus make you every bit whole so His praises are revealed in your life! Hallelujah! 1 Peter 2: 9, NIV says. "But you are a chosen people, a royal priesthood, a holy nation, a people belonging to God, that you may declare the praises *(virtues)* of him who called you out of *(the wisdom of)* darkness into his wonderful *(wisdom of)* light." *(Emphasis Mine)*.

Next, one of the by-products of the work of the Holy Spirit in our life, is changed speech. James says a mature person has learnt to control the tongue, "For in many things we offend all. If any man offend not in word, the same is a perfect *(mature)* man, and able to bridle the whole body." James 3: 2, KJV. He goes on to say that we begin to talk loving, positively constructive, and not negative. "But the tongue can no man tame; it is an unruly evil, full of deadly poison. Therewith, bless we God, even the Father, and therewith curse we men, which are made after the similitude of God. Out of the same mouth proceedeth blessing and cursing. My brethren, these things ought not so to be. Doth a fountain send forth at the same place, sweet water and bitter? Can a fig tree, my brethren, bear olives berries? either a vine figs? So can no fountain both yield salt water and fresh." James 3: 8 – 12, KJV, *(Emphasis Mine*.

A mature person knows his own frailty and speaks truth, health, and encouragement to and about others. Jesus said, "But I tell you that men will have to give account on the day of judgment for every careless word they have spoken. For by your words you will be acquitted and by your words you will be condemned." Matthew 12: 36 – 37, NIV.

God does not teach us to speak anything negative. "... Let no one say when he is tempted, "I am tempted by God," for God cannot be tempted by evil, nor does He himself tempt anyone. But, each one is tempted when he is drawn away by his own desires and enticed. Do not be deceived, my beloved brethren.... Every good gift and every perfect gift is from above, and comes down from the Father of lights, with whom there is no variation of shadow of turning. Of His own will, He brought us forth by the word of truth that we might be a kind of first fruits of His creatures *(new creatures in Christ Jesus – His workmanship created in Christ Jesus)."* James 1: 12 – 18, NKJV, *(Emphasis Mine).*

Two things to be noted in this passage of scripture is that is we are exhorted not to be deceived of where temptation of all types, or to be negative - comes from. Second God brought us forth to be first firsts of His creatures by the wisdom taught in the word of truth about God's character. His word does not teach us to be negative or condemn others for their flaws. It does not teach us to complain about circumstances either.

First God's wisdom teaches us to speak with grace, to be constructive, and positive to and of others or be still. Proverbs 12: 18, NASB says, "There is one who speaks rashly like the thrust of a sword, but the tongue of the wise brings healing."

Everyone needs encouragement. It has been said by some, "Encouragement is oxygen to the soul." "Anxiety in a man's heart weighs it down, but a good word makes it glad." Proverbs 12: 25, NASB. Again, Proverbs says, "A man will be satisfied with good by the fruit of his words. And the deeds of a man's hands will return to him." Proverbs 12: 14, NASB. Our tongue should be wholesome all the time according to James chapter 3: 9 –12. Nothing negative should come out of our mouths. When we learn to speak and live positively, we begin to attract positive relationships and circumstances to us. If we continually speak negative things and behave negatively, we attract negative relationships and circumstances to us, see Proverbs 12: 14 again NASB.

Listen to another scripture in Proverbs "A wholesome tongue is a tree of life, but perverseness in it breaks the spirit." Proverbs 15: 4, NKJV. The NASB reads like this, "A soothing tongue is a tree of life, but perversion in it crushes the spirit." Along with "Death and life are in the power of the tongue, and those who love it will eat its fruit." Proverbs 18: 21, NASB. If we love to wag our tongues, remember we can not take back what we have said once it is out there. You can apologize, but it is still there like, a nail pulled out of a board the nail is gone but the hole is still there. "A brother offended is harder to be won than a strong city, and contentions are like the bars of a citadel." Proverbs 18: 19, NASB.

A mature person knows the danger of the tongue. They use it only when good comes from it. Don't you wish we were all mature – it's like dieting however, when we eat that cookie you promised not to eat, forgive yourself and don't eat anymore. If you speak an unkind word, ask the person to forgive you, God to forgive you, and then forgive yourself. Then purpose not to speak evil again. Becoming mature is a growth and development process. God will send another opportunity to test your commitment. "A man has joy by the answer of his mouth, and a word spoken in due season how good it is!" Proverbs 15: 23. "A word fitly spoken is like apples of gold in settings of silver." Proverbs 25: 11. In other words, it's wonderful to listen to someone who knows what they're talking about or knows the right thing to say at the right time. This includes knowing when to be quiet.

I want to go back to attracting good things into your life. Attitude has a lot to do with the tongue. It is a fact, if you want to change your life, change your attitude and your thoughts will get better too. When the attitude changes, disposition and speech changes. The amazing thing about it is that you choose your attitude. In addition, the Holy Spirit will inspire you to do that also.

The bible tells us this, "All the days *(circumstances)* of the afflicted are bad, but a cheerful heart *(good attitude)* has a continual feast." Proverbs 15: 15, NASB, *(Emphasis Mine)*. Solomon is addressing people who think everything is going south for whatever reason, but if they stay positive, the experience will reveal the abundance of grace coming into their situation. Another favorite attitude scripture of mine is Proverbs 19: 19, "A man of great wrath will suffer punishment; For if you rescue him, you will have to do it again." This is saying that some people think or act as every problem or disagreement with another is a catastrophe. Further, if you intervene to arbitrate or fix it for them you will have to do it again. They have to learn by experience, from the school of hard knocks sometimes, to work through things or they will never grow. Some folks want you to solve their problems, that's not your responsibility. Your responsibility is to encourage and cheer them on in their own efforts to do better. If they'll receive it, they will develop and grow stronger. They may not like you for it until they see the results.

I had a young man in my unit at Fort Gordon that couldn't pass an "Army Physical Fitness Test", out of several that couldn't either. The young man could not do but one pushup and only a couple of situps at the age of nineteen. I ask him, "What did you do at home, did you just sit on the couch all the time and watch TV?" His answer didn't suprise me, he answered, "Yes." I put the whole group on a physical fitness program that started at 4:30 AM every morning. We did pushups and situps, and ran or walked ten miles every morning for two months as they were able. I gave them an incentive to get them to finish the tens miles, running it instead of walking it. The incentive was a hot breakfast opportunity from 6 – 8 AM or and they would have to eat C-rations for breakfast instead of a hot meal. The first three miles were ran with 25 lb. back packs. In two months they all passed the Army PT test. This one soldier came to me afterwards and told me he hated me at first but now he wanted to thank me for what I did for him. Sometimes you have to be firm and loving at the same time for that person or groups good. We were the only unit at that time that didn't have any soldiers on remedial PT. If you got to do something, do it don't play with it.

God wants us to learn to stop feeling defeated every time we have a problem and with His help fix our own problems, knowing that all things work for the good of those who love God and are called according to His purpose. See Romans 8: 28. Problems develop us; we need stress to grow and that is what problems do. People normally withdraw from negative people unless they are negative themselves – misery loves company. Losers always see problems as a defeat before they start analyzing it – winners always see things as opportunity to grow and learn. My son Kevin, when tackling something new, always says, "Oh well let's see what we can learn here." He and his brothers have his mother's patience – I had to learn mine and I'm still learning to be patient – Judy's seems to come natural. I have learnt you don't need to ask for patience, just practice it, there is plenty of opportunity for practice in life.

If you are positive minded and have a positive attitude, you attract better relationships, you marry better, produce more, and have a better quality of life. Every success in life begins with attitude. A positive attitude begins to give you "The Abundant Life" Jesus has for you when you let Him, through the help of the Holy Spirit, renew your mind and change your attitudes and habits. He will renew it into a positive mindset and life style. The journey of learning from Him will set you free from the bondage of a negative mindset and the rewards it has given you.

It has been stealing, killing, and robbing you of the peace and the success that belongs to you and God wants to get it back for you.

It is said "God wants good things for you" and such an assertion is true and backed up by scripture see Matthew 7: 11 and John 10: 10. We have to change the way we think about people and circumstances to attain them. Let us see what Proverbs says about the "Law of Attraction" - "Get wisdom! Get understanding! Do not forget, nor turn away from the words of my mouth, Do not forsake her, and she will preserve you, love her, and she will keep you. Wisdom is the principle thing: Therefore get wisdom, and in your getting, get understanding *(discernment)*. Exalt her, and she will promote you; she will bring you honor, when you embrace her, she will place on your head an ornament of grace; a crown of glory she will deliver to you." Proverbs 4: 5 – 9, NKJV, *(Emphasis Mine)*. Solomon is saying the same thing Jesus said in John 10: 10, "I have come that they might have life and that life more abundant." Wisdom is there saying the same thing and it is yours for the asking and seeking. As you walk in the proper wisdom, you attract abundance to you in positive relationships, health, and prosperity. I like this tidbit of wisdom from Solomon, "A man who has friends must himself be friendly, but there is a friend who sticks closer than a brother." Proverbs 18: 24, NKJV. To become that friendly with some, takes a lot of "humility, gentleness, patience, showing tolerance for one another in love, being diligent to preserve the unity of the Spirit in the bond of peace." Ephesians 4: 2-3, NASB. Abraham Lincoln stated once, "I don't like that man, I must get to know him better." There is something we can like in everyone and build on, Abraham Lincoln seemed to make an effort to find it.

"Let nothing be done through selfish ambition or conceit, but in lowliness of mind let each esteem others better than himself." Philippians 2: 3, NKJV. The wisdom of God teaches servitude coupled with humility, integrity and contentment. Start where you are. See 1 Corinthians 7: 16 – 24 and Ephesians 5: 15 – 17.

Another scripture tells us, "Now, Godliness with contentment is great gain." 1 Timothy 6:6. Paul said in another place, "Not that I speak in respect of want: for I have learned in whatsoever state *(circumstance)* I am therewith to be content. I know how to be abased and I know how to abound: every where and in all things *(circumstances)* I am instructed both to be full and to be hungry, both to abound and to suffer need. I can do all things through Christ who strengtheneth me." Philippians 4: 11 – 13, KJV, *(Emphasis Mine)*. He exhorts the Christians to follow his example in this in 1 Corinthians 7: 16 – 24, NKJV. "... Brethren, let each one remain with God in that state in which he was called." You accept your marriage, your employment and career, whatever state you find yourself in, with contentment and a good attitude. This is a call to being a proactive and faithful in our stewardship. The promise of God is this, you give yourselves to contentment and faithful stewardship in exchange for His help in becoming productive and fruit bearing, "Humble yourselves before the Lord and He will lift you up." James 4: 10, NIV.

How do we humble ourselves in the sight of the Lord? By accepting providence with contentment and a good positive faith filled attitude and assurance of heart in his care and wisdom. It comes from knowing circumstances, and the effort to overcome the infirmities in us, are stepping-stones to our growth. They are to the praise of God's glory as God's purposes of regeneration are accomplished in us. We will become stronger and more adept for endurance. The endurance of our developmental growth process in these circumstances makes us more consistent in behavior. Our circumstances bring about maturity, reading gives knowledge, experience gives wisdom and skillfulness. Use of this wisdom and applying this knowledge through experience produces strength and character – not skill alone! "But refuse profane and old wives' fables, and exercise thyself rather unto godliness." 1 Timothy 4: 7, KJV, let me add – in whatever situation you find yourself, see Proverbs 3: 5 – 6, then you will be exercising godliness.

Let us join in David's example as he prayed, "Let the words of my mouth and the meditation *(thoughts and attitudes)* of my heart be acceptable in thy sight, O Lord, my strength and my Redeemer." Psalm 19: 14, KJV. In every situation, learn, grow, be content, and rejoice always, and you will be fountains of living water making the lives of others rich (see 1 Thessalonians 5: 15 – 23 and 2 Corinthians 6: 10). And, "And let us not be weary in well doing; for in due season we shall reap, if we faint not." Galatians 6: 9, KJV. But as for you, brethren, do not grow weary in doing good *(behaving right)*." 2 Thessalonians 3: 13, NKJV *(Emphasis Mine)*.

Life is a labor of worship to the Lord and a labor of love to our fellow man that accomplishes His sanctifying purposes in us as well. What we become on the journey is more important than what we achieve, for in it is our real reward. "Therefore my beloved brethren, be steadfast, unmovable, always abounding in the work of the Lord, forasmuch as you know that your labor is not in vain in the Lord." 1 Corinthians 15: 58, KJV. We get to labor with God in this world, what a reward, "For we are God's fellow workers; you are God's field, you are God's building." 1 Corinthians 3: 9. You are becoming fountains of living waters to the world and it is comes from walking in the wisdom of the Holy Spirit within you to maturity, See Colossians 4: 5.

CHAPTER V

"THE NEW LIFE PRODUCES SIGNIFICANCE"

Good will and service is a by-product of maturity. Jesus put it this way:

But Jesus called them to Himself and said to them, "You know that those who are considered rulers over the Gentiles lord it over them, and their great ones exercise authority over them. Yet, it shall not be so among you; but whoever desires to become great *(significant)* among you shall be your servant. And whoever of you desires to be first shall be your servant. And whoever of you desires to be first shall be slave of all. For even the Son of Man did not come to be served, but to serve, and to give His life a ransom for many.

Mark 10: 42 – 45, NKJV, *(Emphasis Mine)*.

Abraham Lincoln said this about power and positional leadership, "Nearly all men can stand adversity, but if you want to test a man's character, give him power." If you stop and think about it, where you have worked in the past, most first line supervisors, and some upper echelon leaders are positional leaders only, until they find they do not have the respect of their followers. Then they either make a change or become a political tyrant. Christ teaches servant leadership with character and industries and corporations are searching for more of this type leader everyday. The day of the bully, even in the military, are vanishing, I say vanishing because I recently in the last decade have met a few that excepted change in behavior or the alternative after being put on notice. Some never really change. They are like little Johnny that says after being told to sit down, "I'm sitting down, but I'm standing up on the inside."

Paul led like Jesus and stated that he made himself a servant to all men for their good not his, in 1 Corinthians 9: 19 – 23, "For though I am free from all men, I have made myself a servant to all, that I might win the more; and to the Jews I became as a Jew, that I might win the Jews; to those who are under the law, as under the law, that I might win those who are under the law, that I might win those who are under the law; to those who are without law, as without law (not being without law toward God, but under law toward Christ), that I might win those who are without law; to the weak I became as weak, that I might win the weak, I have become all things to all men, that I might by all means save some. Now this I do for the gospels sake, that I may be partaker of it with you." 1Corinthians 9: 19 – 23, NKJV. See Matthew 9: 37 – 38, and 1 Corinthians 3: 8 – 10.

Let's look at what Paul is saying, Paul had made a statement in 1 Corinthians 8: 1 – 3 earlier that brings more meaning on his statement in chapter 9 about Christian servant-hood, let's look at it:

"Now about food sacrificed to idols; we know that we all have knowledge. Knowledge puffs up but love builds up. The man, who thinks he knows something, does not yet know, as he ought to know. But the man who loves God is known by Him." 1st Corinthians 8: 1 –3, NIV.

Paul in this section of scripture is saying that knowledge can puff us up and can make us religious, positional workers with God. However, real love seeks to serve the edification and welfare of others. They pursue this more than starting sects or posturing for position or titles, which come from religious notions. This comes from a misunderstanding of where our knowledge and skills come from. We have been given these things through revelation of the Spirit, our experiences in life through God's care, as well as the potential we are born with are for serving the welfare of others.

What do I mean by God's care? Everything we receive, according to scripture, even our experiences are from God. Paul asserts this to the Corinthians Christians. "For who makes you differ from another? And what do you have that you did not receive? Now if you did indeed receive it, why do you boast as if you had not received it?" 1 Corinthians 4: 7, NKJV. That is why we are called to acknowledge God in all our affairs in Proverbs 3: 5 – 6. This scripture promises that He will direct our steps, so we are truly here to serve God's purposes and the welfare of others. This is a core belief of the Christian faith and becomes our life style. As this life style evolves it becomes noticeable and fruit producing. (See Matthew 20: 25 – 28).

If God were a positional leader and not a servant leader, so to speak, we would be in big trouble. Here is an example of positional leadership based on power with minimal experience. "And when His disciples, James and John, saw this they said, "Lord, do You want us to command fire to come down from heaven and consume them, just as Elijah did?" But he turned and rebuked them and said, "You do not know what manner of spirit you are of. For the Son of Man did not come to destroy men's lives but to save them." And they went to another village." Luke 9: 55 – 56, NKJV. Thank God, we are under grace and not law, Amen!

Paul saw his position the same as Christ, "For even if I should boast somewhat freely about the authority the Lord gave us for building you up rather than pulling you down. I will not be ashamed of it." 2 Corinthians 10: 8, NIV. We are called to serve not be served.

I think referring to the way Jesus put it in Matthew 9 would help us understand spiritual servant-hood even better here, "As Jesus passed on from there, He saw a man named Matthew sitting at the tax office. And He said to him, "Follow Me." So he arose and followed Him. Now it happened, as Jesus sat at the table in the house, that behold, many tax collectors and sinners came and sat down with Him and His disciples. And when the Pharisees saw it, they said to His disciples, Why does your teacher eat with tax collectors and sinners?" When Jesus heard that, He said to them, "Those who are well have no need of a physician, but those who are sick. But go learn what this means, "I desire mercy and not sacrifice *(religion)*." For I did not come to call the righteous, but sinners to repentance." Matthew 9: 9 – 12, NKJV, *(Emphasis Mine)*.

Jesus knows the potential in everyone of us and like a good coach wants to bring the best out of us without condemning but His working in us through relationship. That relationship is in the person of the Holy Spirit now. He works with all longsuffering, through the Holy Spirit and the preaching and teaching of the gospel to that end, see Hebrews 13: 20 – 21 and 1 Thessalonians 2: 13.

On another time, Jesus had to confront religious attitudes during a time that the disciples were going through the grain fields on the Sabbath and they began to pluck the heads of grain and to eat. Jesus gave this rebuke again, "... But if you had known what this means, I desire mercy and not sacrifice, you would not have condemned the guiltless *(innocent)*." Matthew 12: 1 – 8 *(Emphasis Mine) - read the whole passage)*.

We are to serve the welfare of our brothers and sister's, and our society for their edification and living out of purity of heart. We make allowances, and not being overbearing, or over critical of mistakes or failures. However, we don't tolerate quitting, you quit I quit. I'm not as concerned if someone has failed, but I am concerned when someone is content with their failure. However, if someone is trying to force you to accept something contrary to the core values of Christ, you stand your ground on your convictions.

We are to understand that we are all under development, therefore, we are to be exercising patience, being nonjudgmental, and not being condemning of others. We do call sin - sin however and exercise church discipline when needed. A fellow minister friend of mine, Milford Vaught, has a saying I like to use instead of condemning the unbeliever or a weak brother, "If not for the grace of God that could be me." Nor should we be complaining about people, situations and circumstances. In these times, the fruit of patience and long-suffering are being manifested at their best. Positive minded people are solution oriented and inquisitive searching for solutions, not blame. Paul put this in a prayer for the Colossians. "... being strengthened with all power according to His glorious might so that you may have great endurance and patience and joyfully giving thanks to the Father,...." Colossians 1: 11, NIV.

I am not stating that we give up discernment, but we do stop condemning others to hell for religious differences over liberties, weakness of conscious, slow personal growth, or development as a person. Instead, we concern ourselves with the weightier matters of the law. Not straining at a gnat and swallowing a camel. We are to approach every situation or person with concern for one another's welfare, liberty of conscious, personal growth, and development as a person. Try a little gentleness *(empathy and compassion)*.

The weightier matters of life according to the gospel are to be confronted only in the spirit of seeking to evolve or restore a person. See Galatians 6: 1 – 2. Keep an open mind because you may misunderstand – we are all evolving. You may be tempted in the same area also. "And the servant of the Lord must not quarrel but be gentle to all, able to teach, patient, in humility correcting those who are in opposition. If God perhaps will grant them repentance, so that they may know the truth, and that they may come to their senses and escape the snare of the devil, having been taken captive by him to do his will." - 2 Timothy 2: 24 – 26. And Paul again says, "Brethren, if a man is overtaken in any trespass, you who are spiritual *(mature)* restore such a one in a spirit of gentleness, considering yourself lest you also be tempted. Bear one another's burdens, and so fulfill the law of Christ" Galatians 6: 1 – 2, NKJV. *(Emphasis Mine)*.

If we want to follow the example of Christ, the Apostles and their teaching, we have to pour ourselves out in service toward the growth and welfare others through prayer and example. Being willing to teach with patience, not just by preaching at others. See 1 Peter 5: 2 – 5.

For without good character and fruit of the Spirit, preaching and exhortation are vain. People will learn more from a gentle caring spirit and example than they will from condemning talk. Remember to, "He that has friends must himself be friendly, but there is a friend that sticks closer than a brother." Proverbs 18: 24, NKJV. A real friend will stand by you when you are your worst.

That is what Paul was saying in 1 Corinthians 9: 19 – 23 above, I make myself a servant (friend and example to all men) no matter their background. I make allowances for their background and level of growth. He said it this way to the Philippians. "Yes, and if I am being poured out as a drink offering on the sacrifice and service of your faith. I am glad and rejoice with you all." Philippians 2: 17, NKJV, see Matthew 9: 37 – 38. Another's personal growth and development in applying the creed of the faith, in the entirety of life's affair is serving without becoming high minded as Lord's over your brothers and sisters, see 1 Peter 5: 2 - 3. Again using Paul as an example, for those who had weak consciences, he became weak, for those who were in trespasses; he was gentle and not harsh unless he had to be, see 2 Corinthians 10: 9 - 11.

Paul looked at himself as a debtor to all men and looked for opportunity to serve the gospel to all.

Now I do not want you to be unaware, brethren, that I often planned to come to you (but was hindered until now), that I might have some fruit among you also, just as among the other Gentiles. I am a debtor both to Greeks and to barbarians, both to wise and to unwise. So, as much as is in me, I am ready to preach the gospel to you who are in Rome also. For I am not ashamed of the gospel of Christ, for it is the power of God to salvation for everyone who believes, for the Jew first and also for the Greek.

Romans 1: 13 – 16, NKJV.

Paul saw position and favor as an obligation to serve the good of others, saved or unsaved. When an organization gives you an opportunity at leadership or employment, as Christians it is to serve the welfare of your associates. The organization's welfare should be your highest aim without abusing others, this glorifies God and adorns His teaching. This also attracts honor and favor to yourself, remember the "Law of Attraction" we discussed from Proverbs chapter four above. Thus, "Your will be done on earth even as it is in heaven" as in the Lord's prayer.

Applying this last statement and scripture to the secular part of our life, we find that we are to manifest the life of God to the world around us, habitually! Then we become laborers with God in the harvest, see 1 Corinthians 3: 8 – 14. Jesus asked the disciples to pray for more laborers in the harvest in Matthew 9: 37 – 38, you are called to labor with God in that state in life you find yourself, 1 Corinthians 7: 16 –24. This a call to bloom were you are, what a privilege. This is our reasonable service to God for the mercies shown to us in Christ, See Romans 12: 1 – 2. Paul acknowledged those mercies, making the statement above in Romans 1: 13 – 16.

This new life in us is continually evolving and finding opportunities of being expressed making us God's good seed (laborers) in the world. Jesus explained it this way:

He answered them and said to them. "He who sows the good seed is the Son of Man. The field is the world, the good seeds are the sons of the kingdom, but the tares are the sons of the wicked one. The enemy who sowed them is the devil. The harvest is the end of the age, and the reapers are the angels. Therefore, as the tares are gathered and burned in the fire, so it will be at the end of this age. The Son of Man will cast out His angels, and they will gather out of His kingdom all things that offend and those who practice lawlessness, and will cast them into the furnace of fire. There will be wailing and gnashing of teeth. Then the righteous will shine forth as the sun in the kingdom of their Father. He who has ears to hear let him hear!

Matthew 13: 37 – 43, NKJV.

We are to be good seed (laborers), to the family, work, business, and church. Offenses in any of these areas of life, is an offense to God and His work He is striving to do in the lives of those he has put in your life. We are a debtor to all men that we might bear fruit among them, see 1 Corinthians 10: 31 – 33 and Matthew 5: 16.

Paul illustrates by example what he considers a debtor or servant to all men's welfare in this passage of scripture.

For if we are beside ourselves, it is for God, or if we are of sound mind, it is for you. For the love of Christ, compels us, because we judge thus; that if One died for all, then all died *(became debtors)*; and He died for all, that those who live should no longer live for themselves *(but for others for His name sake)*, but for Him (by showing His love and faithfulness to family, employer, co-workers, business relations, and church members) who died for them and rose again.

2 Corinthians 5: 13 – 15, NKJV, *(Emphasis Mine)*.

John puts it like this in 1 John;

Hereby perceive we the love of God, because he laid down his life for us: and we ought to lay down our lives for the brethren.

1 John 3: 16 KJV.

This laying of our life down for others is fulfilled when we fulfill this passage in Galatians, "And those who are Christ's have crucified - *(surrendered their desires to do His will)*, the flesh with its passions and desires." Galatians 5: 24, NKJV, (Emphasis Mine). Your life consists of your ambitions and desires. By surrendering them for the pursuit of what honors God, and the benefit of others - you lay down your life *(your passions and desires)* offering it a holy living sacrifice.

Paul said, "... I die daily." See 1 Corinthians 15: 31. What did he die daily too? He gave his passions and desires up for what honored God through his behavior. He served what was best for those that were working with him and those he was ministering too, that he might have some fruit among them in his life. He poured himself, emptied himself of what rights he had to become a servant to purposely serve the welfare and edification of those he was laboring to save.

It is peculiar that John 3: 16, when talking about the sacrifice of God's only begotten Son, and 1 John 3: 16, also talks about the sacrifice to be made by all Saints for others, have the same street address and are in different books of the Bible. I believe the Holy Spirit did this on purpose. Just as Christ laid down His life - He calls us to lay down our life for the welfare of the brethren in the same way. "... (Verse: 27). As the Son of Man did not come to be served, but to serve, and to give His life a ransom for many...." Matthew 20: 25 – 28, we are to follow His example. And again "Let not each of you look out not only for his own interest, but in lowliness of mind let each esteem others better than himself." Philippians 2: 4, see 1 Corinthians 19 – 23. Another way to apply this new life of love is in Romans. In Romans 15, Paul explains it in this way,

We then who are strong ought to bear with the scruples of the weak, and not to please (serve) ourselves. Let each of us please (serve) his neighbor for his good, leading to edification. For even Christ did not please (serve) Himself; but as it is written, "The reproaches of those who reproached You fell on Me. For whatever things were written before were written for our learning. Now may the God of patience and comfort grant you to be like-minded toward one another, according to Christ Jesus. Therefore receive one another, just as Christ also received us, to the glory of God.

Romans 15: 1 – 7, NKJV.

This is the most important service you render to one another. It is not just menial tasks; it is a loving example coupled with listening friendship willing to sacrifice, ready to edify, encourage and comfort one another. Some say they will not attend church because it is full of hypocrites. It may seem that way at times, but in actuality, it is full of developing saints striving for perfection though living in an imperfect world due to the tainting of sin and Satan. Even though there are tares there, what is that to you, go feed among my lambs.

Paul commands us several times to comfort and edify one another throughout scripture, let us look at a couple. "Therefore do not let your good be spoken of as evil; for the kingdom of God is not eating and drinking, but righteousness and peace and joy in the Holy Spirit. For he who serves Christ in these things is acceptable to God and approved by men. Therefore, let us pursue the things that make for peace and the things by which one may edify another. Do not destroy the work of God for the sake of food. All things indeed are pure, but it is evil for the man who eats with offense." Romans 14: 16 – 19, NKJV.

A good example goes a long way so does a bad one. This does not just mean only what we eat or drink, but all that we do (See 1 Corinthians 10: 31 - 33). Another scripture about edifying behavior goes like this, "Therefore comfort each other and edify one another just as you also are doing." 1 Thessalonians 5: 11, NKJV. Nothing is more edifying than a good example or mentor, Paul was that and one you could look up to. I think Billy Graham is another one that rose in this generation that can be looked up to - among others.

It seems the gospel calls us to choose our battles carefully. There are some things we just do not argue over if it is just a matter of conscience concerning liberty, do not offend your brothers' conscience if it makes him offend. (See 1 Corinthians 10: 21 – 24, 31 – 33, & Romans 14: 21). The weightier matters of the law are more important than claiming our liberty in Christ. "For you brethren have been called to liberty; only do not use liberty as an opportunity to the flesh, but through love serve one another. For all the law is fulfilled in one word, even in this: "You shall love your neighbor as yourself." But if you bite and devour one another, beware lest you be consumed of one another!" See Galatians 5: 13 -15, NKJV. 1 Corinthians 8: 1, says love edifies, this means love seeks with the purpose of being a good example and a mentor of grace.

Finally then let us walk as being acceptable to the Lord. Another way Paul puts it is in Ephesians. "I therefore, the prisoner of the Lord, beseech you to walk worthy of the calling with which you were called, with all lowliness, and gentleness, with longsuffering, bearing with one another in love, endeavoring to keep the unity of the Spirit in the bond of peace." Ephesians 4: 1 – 3, NKJV. Just as Jesus said it, "Blessed are the peace makers for they shall be called sons of God." Matthew 5: 9. This is serving others... I do not need to cut your grass, give you money as much as I need to have good character before God and man, for your edification, Gods' glory and my sake. Therefore, let us put on love, the bond of perfection, as asserted to in Colossians 3: 14. As we can see in our fellowships our seeking peace and what edifies is important to God. What edifies is exemplary behavior. So as we become part of a congregation and begin to mature we will seek to live a life in decency and ordered in godly behavior, working to keep the unity of the spirit in the bond of peace. (See Ephesians 4: 1 – 3 & and 1 Corinthians 14: 40), Read the whole chapter, you will see how it fits with this chapter. Also read 1 Corinthians 13. A good example is the best legacy you could leave to this life.

The church's mandate for caring for one another comes from Jesus himself, "But whoever causes one of these little ones who believe in Me to sin. It would be better for him if a millstone were hung around his neck, and he were drowned in the depth of the sea." Matthew 18: 6, NKJV. Verse 14 says, "Even so it is not the will of your Father who is in heaven that one of these little ones should perish." Another warning in chapter 18, verse 10 –11, NKJV, goes like this, "Take heed that you do not despise one of these little ones. For I say to you that in heaven, their angels always see the face of My Father who is in heaven. For the Son of Man has come to save that which was lost."

Let me finish this chapter with this, "Therefore receive one another, just as Christ also received us, to the glory of God," Romans 15: 7. Seek to be an encourager, a comforter *(nothing comforts more than a good listener or a good word of encouragement)* and example to others. Look for good mentors in the faith such as Pastors, other growing Christians to imitate, see 1 Corinthians 11: 1. Also, in your secular careers, leaders and co-workers that will help you grow in the faith and in your careers and produce Christian virtues and good work ethics. A good example goes a long way and has influence.

CHAPTER VI

"The New Life Evolves to Resting in God"

There remaineth therefore a rest to the people of God. Hebrews 4: 9, KJV.

Now we look into this rest that God has given us and called His people to, and to get an understanding of what it means to wait upon God. The new life we have is also, a life of waiting upon God. A Christian is told to be anxious for nothing. "Be anxious for nothing, but in everything by prayer and supplication, with thanksgiving, let your request be known to God; and the peace of God, which surpasses understanding, will guard your hearts and minds through Christ Jesus." Philippians 4: 6 – 7. In the next few pages, we will see why. First, I want to lay out a foundation of scriptures for study to bring us to an understanding of the control God's has over providence and the dispensation of time.

"But one testified in a certain place, saying:

What is man that You are mindful of him, or the son of man that You take care of him? You have made him a little lower than the angels; You have crowned him with glory and honor, and set him over the works of Your hands. You have put all things in subjection under his feet." For in that He put all in subjection under him, He left nothing that is not under him. But now we do not yet see all things put under him. But, we see Jesus, who was made a little lower than the angels, for the suffering of death, crowned with glory and honor, that He, by the grace of God, might taste death for everyone.

Hebrews 2: 6 – 9, NKJV.

We see Jesus seated on the right hand of the Father waiting for the joy that was set before Him, this joy is a promise that He would inherit a Kingdom of which He is Lord and His kingdom will never perish. He has inherited it and waits for the total fulfillment of it as explained in 1 Corinthians 15: 20 – 24. In addition, Ephesians alludes to it, "which He worked in Christ when He raised Him from the dead and seated Him at His right hand in the heavenly places." Ephesians 1: 20, NKJV. Now let us go further in this inheritance of living the life of God.

"Seeing then that we have a great High Priest who has passed through the heavens, Jesus the Son of God, let us hold fast our confession. For we do not have a high priest, who cannot sympathize with our weaknesses, but was in all points tempted as we are, yet without sin. Let us therefore come boldly to the throne of grace, that we may obtain mercy and find grace to help in the time of need." Hebrews 4: 14 –16, NKJV.

"But God who is rich in mercy, because of His great love with which He loved us, even when we were dead in trespasses, made us alive together with Christ (by grace you have been saved), and raised us up together and made us sit together in the heavenly places in Christ Jesus that in the ages to come He might show the exceeding riches of His grace in His kindness toward us in Christ Jesus." Ephesians 2: 4 – 7, NKJV.

Knowing we have been made to sit with Christ in heavenly places is important to understanding our position in Christ and the terminology "Rest of God" and of waiting upon God for the working of His power toward us who believe.

Beginning at verse 19, "... and what is the exceeding greatness of His power toward us who believe, according to the working of His mighty power which He worked in Christ when He raised Him from the dead and seated Him at His right hand in the heavenly places, far above all principality and power and might and dominion, and every name that is named, not only in this age but also in that which is to come. And He put all things under His feet, and gave Him to be head over all things to the church, which is His body, the fullness of Him who fills all in all." Ephesians 1: 15, 19 – 23, NKJV.

Our salvation was planned from the beginning of the age. And now the church is the fullness of His presence on earth. Even though Jesus said there would be tares in the church, He still resides over the church services and manifest himself in different ways in those services. "To me who am less than the least of all the saints, this grace was given, that I should preach among the Gentiles the unsearchable riches of Christ, and to make all see what is the fellowship of the mystery, which from the beginning of the ages has been hidden in God who created all things through Jesus Christ; to the intent that now the manifold wisdom of God might be made known by the church to the principalities and powers in heavenly places, according to the eternal purpose which He accomplished in Christ Jesus our Lord." Ephesians 2: 8 – 11, NKJV. Now listen what God said about the Sabbath.

Thus the heavens and the earth, and all the host of them, were finished. And on the seventh day God ended His work which He had done and He rested on the seventh day from all

His work which He had done." Then God blessed the seventh day and sanctified it, because in it He rested from all His work which God had created and made.

See Genesis 2: 1 – 3, NKJV.

Now God's rest is spoken of in the New Testament. We find that we are to enter this same rest as though everything is finished leaving our struggles in His care, knowing we are kept until that day. That's why we are identified as sitting at the right hand of the Father in Jesus in Ephesians 2: 4 – 7 quoted above. We are to accept it as a fact now, even though, we still go through trials and temptations. We are maintain a position of sitting in heavenly places in Christ till His work unfolds in its' conclusion. We can know that we are those "... who are kept by the power of God through faith (in this finished work) for salvation ready to revealed in that day, according to 1 Peter 1: 5, see Ephesians 1: 19 again. God is not working out a plan, He all ready knows how the plan works out. He knows the end from the beginning. Just like drawing up a set of blueprints and then given to the builders to do the construction work. It all happens according to the plans on the blueprint. This is what sitting in heaven with Christ means, waiting on God while His purposes unfold in our life and the worlds.

For He has spoken in a certain place of the seventh day in the way: "And God rested on the seventh day from all His works"; and again in this place, "They shall not enter My rest." Since therefore it remains that some must enter it, and those to whom it was first preached did not enter because of disobedience, again He designates a certain day, saying in David, Today after such a long time, as it has been said: "Today, if you will hear His voice, Do not harden your hearts." For if Joshua had given them rest, then He would not afterward have spoken of another day. There remains therefore a rest for the people of God. *(Verse 9)* For he who has entered His rest has himself also ceased from his works as God did from His. Let us therefore be diligent to enter that rest, lest anyone fall according to the same example of disobedience.

Hebrews 4: 4 – 11, NKJV, (Emphasis Mine).

By faith we understand that the worlds were framed by the word of God, so that the things which are seen were not made of things which are visible.

Hebrews 11: 3, NKJV.

The Greek word aiones or aeons means ages. Therefore, God has made the ages. We were created to be in the appointed time or age in the beginning of Creation by God. We are living in the age or generation we are meant to be in. God knew about us before time began and He has a plan and a purpose for us all. Paul made this statement about creation;

And He has made from one blood every nation of men to dwell on all the face of the earth, and has determined their preappointed times and the boundaries of their dwellings, so that they should seek the Lord, in hope that they might grope for Him and find Him, though He is not far from each one of us; for in Him we live and move and have our being, as also some of your own poets have said, "For we also are His offspring".

Acts 17: 26 – 28, NKJV.

All these scriptures indicate that God's work of creation and salvation, beginning to end is finished. It is like taking a blueprint of a house and everything is laid out from beginning to end. The architect knows the end before the beginning. God the architect of the universe and the ages knows the end from the beginning and the in-betweens. We are called to rest by faith in the fact that it is finished and we are called to rest in Him by waiting as His times and His purposes are fulfilled which is only in His keeping and knowing, see Acts 1: 7. He is our rest from worrying about our affairs casting our cares on Him until He reveals the finished product in the day of the Lord Jesus Christ. His work started in the beginning and it is continuing to unfold. We are part of it. It will continue until it will be consummated with the resurrection of the dead, the judgment seat of Christ, the millennial reign of Christ, the second judgment, and the new heavens and earth see 1 Corinthians 15: 24 – 28 and John 1: 1 - 4.

This is how Paul puts it in Ephesians 2: 6, "and raised us up together and made us sit together in the heavenly places in Christ Jesus." He is explaining this waiting on God in light of Hebrews 2: 6 – 9 quoted above. Verse 8 - 9, "You have put all things in subjection under his feet. For in that He put all in subjection under him, He left nothing that is not put under him. But we see Jesus..." We are sitting with Him in heavenly places, signifying we are waiting on God with Him till all things are put under His feet. The last enemy to be defeated is Death and the Grave, see 1 Corinthians 15: 53 - 57.

First, Christ was and is the cornerstone of God's plan of creation and the purchase of our salvation. Remember God proclaims He knows the end from the beginning, why because all His works are designed by Him, we are are waiting for the finished outcome by faith as Abraham did. All that is needed now is a confident rest or waiting on God in obedience to Him until the times are fulfilled that God had already appointed in His plans from the beginning of creation. How? He created the dispensation of time and therefore He knows and sees the end from the beginning and knows how each generation is going to unfold and end. Therefore, the times and seasons of all events are in His care and He is able to bring His plans to pass. Look at this proceeding scripture with me that indicates God created time again.

"And He has made from one blood every nation of men to dwell on all the face of the earth, and has determined their pre-appointed times and the boundaries of their dwellings, so that they should seek the Lord, in the hope that they might grope for Him and find Him, though He is not far from each one of us; for in Him we live and move and have our being, as also some of your own poets have said, "For we are also His offspring." Acts 17: 26 – 28, NKJV.

Therefore time and eternity are separate but intertwined and God who rested from all His works also rested from creating our times and knows how it plays out, (See Psalm 139: 16, Isaiah 46: 10, Revelation 21: 6, & 22:13).

He knows our time of birth and time of death and the betweentimes, according the Psalms, "your eyes saw my unformed body. All the days ordained for me were written in your book before one of them came to be." Psalm 139: 16, NIV.

God finished His work of Creation on the sixth day. He rested from all His works on the seventh day, this included the plan of salvation and its' time of revealing even to the time of the New Heavens and New Earth. In this dispensation of age in time and eternity, Christ is at the right hand of the Father waiting the appointed time for Him to come to bring his church home, that only the Father knows (see Mark 13: 32). In Acts, The disciples asked Jesus, after He resurrected, this question, "Therefore, when they had come together, they asked Him, saying, "Lord will You at this time restore the kingdom to Israel?" And He said to them, "It is not for you to know times or seasons which the Father has put in His own authority", Acts 1: 6 – 7, NKJV.

See also Matthew 24: 36, and 1 Thessalonians 5: 1 – 2. It is for you to trust.

Through Hebrews chapter four also chapter three, comes a call to enter God's rest. This is having faith in His finished work, and to work out our salvation with God, to evolve into His image as subscribed to in Philippians 2: 12 - 13. This does not give us a license to sin, it gives us faith to labor knowing that our labor is not in vain in the Lord, see 1 Corinthians 15: 58. We do this by His grace that is working in our lives unto good works until He comes, see Ephesians 2: 10 again. This rest is given to the church and each saint and we are commanded to enter in to it. In other words we are to rest in faithfulness, waiting upon His call to come up here. In addition, it is a rest that is to be entered into everyday for the rest of your life. It is called waiting by faith on God's purposes for our life to be worked out in our daily circumstances. You have to enter it by exercising your faith and if not we can end up like the children in the wilderness. God swore that the children of Israel would not enter His rest due to unbelief. He was saying they would not inherit the good He had planned for those that would enter this rest of waiting on Him in every situation. Therefore, they lost out in the wilderness and this life and in the life to come to what extent, we don't know, judgment is God's. "Therefore, since a promise remains of entering His rest, let us fear lest any of you seem to have come short of it. For indeed the gospel was preached to us as well as to them; but the word which they heard did not profit them, not being mixed with faith in those who heard it. For we who have believed do enter that rest, as He has said: "So I swore in My wrath, they shall not enter My rest." Although the works were finished from the foundation of the world." Hebrews 4: 1 – 3. Paul understood this rest when he prayed for the Thessalonians:

Therefore we also pray always for you that our God would count you worthy of this calling, and of His goodness and the work of faith with power, that the name of Christ may be glorified in you, and you in Him, according to the grace of our God and the Lord Jesus Christ.

2 Thessalonians 1: 11 – 12, NKJV.

Paul was praying that they would be counted worthy of entering His rest by working in them faith with power that trusts and waits in obedience. Since Genesis chapter three around six thousand years ago they were to rest and wait on God, and a promise of that rest still remains to us today because He says in verses 6 –11.

Since therefore, it remains that some must enter it; and those to whom it was first preached did not enter because of disobedience, again He designates a certain day, saying in David, Today after such a long time, as has been said: "Today, if you will hear His voice, Do not harden your hearts". For if Joshua had given them rest, then He would not afterward have spoken of another day. There remains therefore a rest for the people of God. For he who has entered His rest has himself also ceased from his works as God did from His. Let us therefore be diligent to enter that rest, lest anyone fall according to the same example of disobedience.

Hebrews 4: 6 – 11, NKJV.

It comes from knowing and having a relationship with God that the Hebrew children were meant to have, but refused in unbelief to obey God. God's faithfulness to His plan and your keeping is as sure as the sunrise.

Romans 5: 1 – 5 describes this relationship, "Therefore having been justified by faith, we have peace with God through our Lord Jesus Christ, through whom also we have access by faith into this grace in which we stand, and rejoice in hope of the glory of God, and not only that, but we also glory in tribulations, knowing that tribulation produces perseverance; and perseverance character, and character, hope. Now hope does not disappoint, because the love of God has been poured out in our hearts by the Holy Spirit who was given to us."

Romans 5: 1 – 5, NKJV.

This fellowship with Him who created everything in heaven and earth including the times and seasons, inspires us to love Him who first loved us. It motivates us to purify ourselves even as He is pure, see I John 3: 3, that we can stay in fellowship and finally live forever in His presence.

Moreover, as God's plan is unfolded right up to the consummation of the age, we are to rest in the fact that God has had a purpose and a plan for our life right from the beginning. This rest is a confidence that what He has promised to happen will happen, and he knows how to fulfill the purposes for our life if we trust Him. He will keep us safe while it is unfolding.

We also believe we have an inheritance of a better world through His grace and kindness wherein dwells only good and righteousness. "This New Earth and New Heaven" we will inherit if His life and image continue to mature in us to the full stature and measure of Jesus Christ. That happens by the choice of living the new life we have commanded to learn and live. We will share in His glory if we continue steadfastly walking in the faith and doctrine of Jesus Christ. This calls for living His life here in this world resting in Him through faith and patience knowing the work is done and that we are only on a journey to develop this image in us. It is asserted in Hebrews: 10: 35 – 39,

Therefore do not cast away your confidence, which has great reward. For you have need of endurance, so that after you He done the will of God, you may receive the promise: "For yet a little while, and He who is coming will come and will not tarry, Now the just shall live by faith; but if anyone draws back, My soul has no pleasure in him." But we are not of those who draw back to perdition, but of those who believe to the saving of the soul.

Hebrews 10: 35 – 39, NKJV.

He tells us, only He knows what tomorrow will bring. This teaches that we are to trust God with tomorrow and walk in faithfulness today.

Come now, you who say, "Today or tomorrow we will go to such and such a city, spend a year there, buy and sell, and make a profit"; whereas you do not know what will happen tomorrow. For what is your life? It is even a vapor that appears for a little time and then vanishes away. Instead, you ought to say, "If the Lord wills, we shall live and do this or that." But now you boast in your arrogance. All such boasting is evil. Therefore, to him who knows to do good and does not do it, to him it is sin.

James 4: 13 – 17, NKJV.

What is this good we know? It is knowing to humble ourselves to acknowledge that He is in control not us and rest in Him as He unfolds His will for our life and brings His purposes to past in us as we seek Him. God knows tomorrow because He knows the end from the beginning. God has promised to keep His people through this life and into the next if they are faithful to Him. "Therefore let those who suffer according to the will of

God, commit their souls to Him in doing good, as to a faithful Creator." 1 Peter 4: 19, NKJV.

In addition, through faith in His care, obedience to His values and principles of true righteousness and holiness *(wholesomeness)*, we are changing into His image and nature from glory to glory. This happens only as we meditate and act on the teaching of His principles making them our core values as by the teaching of the Spirit of the Lord, (See 2 Corinthians 3: 18). There is a dependence on the presence and guidance of the Holy Spirit. Although we enter His rest, we need to stay in it by prayer as Jesus instructed for more grace. See the whole Lord's prayer Luke 11: 2 – 4.

"Another Discipline to Live This Life"

Gods' people have another helper available through prayer, and meditation of the word. Prayer and fasting is another discipline of the faith that Jesus taught and practiced. "As He also says in another place:

You are a priest forever according to the order of Melchizedek." Who, in the days of His flesh, when He had offered up prayers and supplications, with vehement cries and tears to Him who was able to save Him from death, and was heard because of His godly fear, though He was a Son, yet He learned obedience by the things he suffered. And having been perfected, He became the author of eternal salvation to all who obey Him.

Hebrews 5: 6 – 9, NKJV.

Jesus received more anointing for ministry through practicing the disciplines of our faith, prayer and fasting. See Matthew 4: 1 – 17. The new life leads to a life of prayer: "But you beloved, building yourselves up on our most holy faith, praying in the Holy Spirit," Jude 20, NKJV. Jesus and the Apostles spoke and exhorted much on prayer. Prayer builds you up. Paul put it this way, when discussing praying in the Spirit, "He who speaks in a tongue edifies himself, but he who prophesies edifies the church." 1 Corinthians 14: 4, NKJV. In addition, when he finishes on this subject in chapter 14: 13 – 15, NKJV, "Therefore let him who speaks in a tongue pray that he may interpret. For if I pray in a tongue, my spirit prays, but my understanding is unfruitful. What is the conclusion then? I will pray with the spirit, and I will also pray with the understanding, I will sing with the spirit, and I will also sing with the understanding."

Prayer cultivates a relationship with God and access to Him is available to us by faith in Jesus Christ. We are exhorted to come boldly to the throne of His grace to receive grace, mercy, and answers from God in the time of need, see Hebrews 4: 14 – 16. We are to look to God for spiritual wisdom and understanding from God's gracious Holy Spirit making us wise in the scriptures as we rest in Him for the fulfillment of scripture. (See Colossians 3: 16, Ephesians 1: 17, and Romans 15: 4). As we spend time with God in prayer, yearning for Him, the Holy Spirit begins to use those times to speak to our hearts in audible ways to lead and guide us into the truth we need.

When stressed or overwhelmed the faith encourages prayer. It edifies in the things and nature of God, creating His image in us and His life style and personality through His peace. Prayer also receives resources from God for daily needs. His image in us is positive and it gives off positive energy. Love is positive energy! Prayer supplies strength, resources and miracles, prayer and God's word is the life line and blood of the spirit for a Christian.

In addition, He teaches us His ethics through studying His word. I want everyone to know, God is interested in everything about his people and guides them. "The steps of a good man are ordered by the Lord, and He delights in his way. Though he fall, he shall not be utterly cast down; for the Lord upholds him with his hand." In addition, "Let your conduct be without covetousness; be content with such things as you have. For He Himself has said "I will never leave you nor forsake you. So, we may boldly say; the Lord is my helper I will not fear: what can man do to me?" Psalm 37: 23 – 24 & Hebrews 13: 5 – 6, NKJV.

According to the Apostle Luke we are not to get overcharged with this world - leaving prayer out, being over charged with the care and pleasures of life is leaving God out. When we leave God out we will definitely stop praying unless in trouble, and that's not fellowship. That's like someone that comes to our door everytime they are in need and you don't see them again till the next problem.

But take heed to yourselves, lest your hearts be weighed down with carousing, drunkenness, and cares of this life, and that Day come on you unexpectedly... "Watch therefore, and pray always that you may be accounted worthy to escape all these things that will come to pass, and to stand before the Son of Man.

Luke 21: 34 – 36., NKJV.

Paul put it this way in Colossians:

Continue earnestly in prayer, being vigilant in it with thanks giving." Paraphrased he is saying, "Handle life with prayer, vigilantly, watching over every affair.

Colossians 4: 2, NKJV.

Why, prayer activates the power of God through fellowship and stirs our faith in Him. The Lord's prayer covers everything that is required in a day.

Our Father who in heaven hallowed be thy name - *(Worship)*, Your kingdom come, Your will be done on earth as it is in heaven – *(direction, purpose, and revival, maturity in His image)*. Give us day by day our daily bread – *(resources)*. And forgive us our sins, for we also forgive everyone who is indebted to us – *(forgiveness)*. And do not lead us into temptation but deliver us from the evil one – *(protection)* These are the things we are told to ask for in prayer and I believe in that order.

Luke 11: 2 – 4, NKJV, *(Emphasis Mine)*

These are the things we are told to pray for in prayer. As 1 Peter says, "Therefore humble yourselves under the mighty hand of God, that He may exalt you in due time, casting all your care upon Him, for He cares for you. Be sober; be vigilant, because your adversary the devil walks about like a roaring lion, seeking whom he may devour. Resist him steadfast in the faith, knowing that the same sufferings are experienced by your brotherhood in the world." 1 Peter 5: 6 – 9, NKJV

Meditation is another discipline that is not to be neglected. Prayer is the most important part of our day. It really is! God uses prayer and the word as a vehicle for us to receive because He created us to depend on Him. He will give His glory to no other and that is why He insists on our seeking Him through prayer and feeding our spirits on His word while waiting on Him. In addition, He created us with reason, logic, and recall ability that we could learn from fellowshipping with Him to become positive loving creatures. This journey through this world is the development stage of our eternal self – good or evil.

We pervert His purpose of us conforming to His image with our own negative thoughts and energy. Meditation and prayer in the word helps correct this. Meditating on anything good can do this, which Paul advocated in Philippians 4: 8.

James also backs this up, "Let no one say when he is tempted, "I am tempted by God", for God cannot be tempted by evil, nor does He Himself tempt anyone. But each one is tempted when he is drawn away *(attracted)* by his own desires *(thoughts)* and enticed *(attracted)*." James 1: 13 – 14. Thus "The Law of Attraction" is real in the sense that what we desire most when opportunity comes the subconscious mind has been trained to recognize it. Then what we long for, we gravitate to it.

"Do not be deceived, my beloved brethren, every good gift and every perfect gift is from above, and comes down from the Father of lights, with whom, there is no variation or shadow of turning. Of His own will He brought us forth by the word of truth, that we might be a kind of first fruits of His creatures." James 1: 16 – 17. Everything positive comes from God and there is nothing negative in Him. "This is the message which we have heard from Him and declare to you, that God is light and in Him is no darkness at all." 1 John 1: 5. God doesn't tempt us to be negative it has become a habit from the old life for some.

Solomon taught positive thinking, Proverbs 15: 15, "All the days of the afflicted are evil *(A cup half empty philosophy)*, But he who is of a merry heart *(A cup half full philosophy)* has a continual feast." Proverbs 15: 15, NKJV, *(Emphasis Mine)*. This teaches us not to consider the impossibilities, but the possibilities, not to limit God or ourselves. He also asserted that if a person was habitually negative you could not help them. "A man of great wrath will suffer punishment; for if you rescue him, you will have to do it again." Proverbs 19: 19, NKJV. He even asserted that it was not healthy to be negative, "A merry heart does good, like medicine, but a broken spirit dries the bones." Proverbs 17: 22. Isn't that what modern experts say also, the bible backs them up. Again, "A merry heart makes a cheerful countenance, but by sorrow of the heart the spirit is broken." Proverbs 15: 13. I am going to close this paragraph with this, "Anxiety in the heart of man causes depression, but a good word makes it glad." Proverbs 12: 25. In the words of Abraham Lincoln, "A man is about as happy as he makes up his mind to be." Make up your mind to be happy – "It's Gods' way - Joy!"

The whole conclusion of the matter is that Christians are called to rest in God - casting all their cares on Him through prayer - and waiting on His purposes to be fulfilled through patience - for He cares for us. So, "Rejoice in the Lord always, again I will say rejoice" See Philippians 4: 4, NKJV.

(See 1 Peter 5: 6 –7). This humbling ourselves to Him is being content in whatever state we are in in life and going to Him continually in prayer casting our concerns on Him. Our concerns should consist of what is according to the Lords' prayer above. Let us seek His honor, revival and grace for the soul, forgiveness of sins and our churches and nation, daily resources, and protection. Then wait in obedience, resisting Satan firm in the teaching of the faith, resting in His promises of answered prayer – there is a book full of them! See Hosea 12: 6.

CHAPTER VII

"The New Life Gives Purpose"

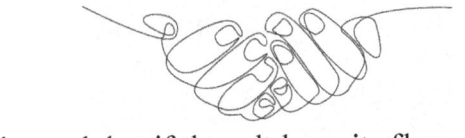

"Salt is good, but if the salt loses its flavor, how will you season it? Have salt *(purpose or commitment)* in yourselves, and have peace with one another." Mark 9: 50, NKJV. *(Emphasis Mine)*.

"A desire accomplished is sweet to the soul, but it is an abomination to fools to depart from evil." Proverbs 13: 19, NKJV.

To have salt is to have purpose and commitment, not living aimlessly but with purpose. Our first purpose as Paul's was with what we have received from the Lord, is to bear fruit among those in our world bringing glory to God. "Now I do not want you to be unaware, brethren that I often planned to come to you (but was hindered till now), that I might have some fruit among you also, just as among the other Gentiles." See Romans 1: 13, NKJV.

It will lead us also to living with a definite purpose that contributes to others and supplies satisfaction and fulfillment to our own life. It also leads to not letting things happen to you because we live passively. With God's help, we become a purposeful people, which is a choice and a decision we make. We develop into disciplined time managers and problem solving individuals instead of whiners. We begin to see, having purpose gives meaning to life. We see we are not only more happy but becoming successful at life, if we make goals and live purposely. To fulfill our potential and to influence as many souls as we can along life's journey, seeking their welfare through example and mentoring servitude. A purpose or goal that fulfills a God given dream, a desire that sows good seed into society and fills a need and helps us grow to our full potential is pleasing to God.

Being purposeful means taking charge of your life and moving forward to fulfill the purpose you feel God has planned for your life. I believe God intended for us to conquerors! As George Bernard Shaw said we should be,"...a force of nature instead of a feverish selfish little clod of ailments and grievances complaining that the world will not devote itself to making you happy." We plan, dream and look for and meditate on opportunity to fulfill our purpose from sharing our faith to fulfilling our God given vision, dream, that passion we seem to have had since birth. Opportunities happen all the time.

"Most people see what is, and never see what can be."
Albert Einstein.

Jesus called for commitment from His followers and so will our goals. This commitment involves living on purpose for God for the rest of our life in all that we do. Whatever the cost, mature Saints are willing to pay the price of living to the glory of God, that price is commitment. We live for His glory in the home, on the job, in ours careers, in the church, anywhere else life and our God given goals takes us. This is seeking to bear fruit among those with us as we journey though life with them. As we begin to serve God, He teaches that life is a stewardship and He opens opportunities that reveal our purpose and sometimes He speaks those purposes to us. It would be good stewardship if we had a purpose statement for family, health, finances, work, career, business, and our worshipful service to God, stewardship entails all of these areas, see 1 Corinthians 4: 1 - 2.

People think of the new life as unachievable and that they can not have a fun life. Some feel they cannot have a dream and live it, but nothing could be more untrue. That is because we don't understand the parables of the talents in Matthew 25: 14 – 30, God does not want us to be useless. These abilities in verse 15, are the potentials and possibilities of our dreams in life. Lord you gave me five dreams and they were accomplished and I dreamed five more and accomplished them also. Well done good and faithful servant but cast the unprofitable servant who hid his dream into a life of vanity and fear, Let him work for someone else who will dare to dream, see also Psalms78: 32 – 33.

The possibilities are the desires of the things we would like to accomplish with our life. Possibilities are the things that can be if we will pay the price, the price is commitment. The question is do we have the salt. As we grow in Christ, our dreams, our purpose will be revealed, become more progressive and fulfilling; some never do grow to this point to realize the abundant life Christ wills for us to live. Due to a lack of faith in God's love and possibly an ignorance of the life of God, "they see things only as they are, not as they could be," as Albert Einstein asserted, see Psalm 78: 32 – 33 again. God wills for us to prosper even as our soul prospers in this life, see 3 John 2. Why do I say abilities are dreams in this scripture? You were born with an undeveloped subconscious, you create its' memories and desires as you develop. God gave us an imagination to use. We use it to create our life and our personality.

Life is not about finding yourself, it is about creating yourself.

George Bernard Shaw.

Dare to dream for you will never go any higher than your aspirations. It is a terrible thing to have no vision.

Helen Keller.

Some begin to talk their selves out of their dream. Some settle for the status quo, "this is the way it has always been". In Japan, the word Kaizan stands for constant improvement. A relationship with Christ brings this kind of purpose to your life. If, "The New Life" is evolving in an individual, it teaches diligence in every area of our personal life from prayer, to family, to work, career, and business, to worship. The new life teaches us to live our life on purpose and our dreams, without leaving the weightier matters of the law undone – living out the core values taught in God's word in all areas of life. Goals stretch us giving us a target we can see. Plans to reach that goal - give us discipline and strategy. Knowing we are being stretched into the image of Christ gives us motivation to exercise integrity and self-discipline in all areas of life. We will then accomplish our goals to the glory of God. Living in the present, we are bearing fruit along the journey to God's glory. It is not what you achieve but what your journey of achievement does in you – the evolving of this new life in you is most important. Proving faithful is, "I have fought the good faith, I have finished the race, and I have kept the faith." 2 Timothy 4: 7. If you leave God out, nothing you accomplish matters.

God gave Joshua a vision and instructions how to fulfill his purpose in Joshua:

After the death of Moses the servant of the Lord, it came to pass that the Lord spoke to Joshua the son of Nun, Moses assistant saying: Moses my servant is dead. Now therefore, arise; go over this Jordan, you and all this people, to the land, which I am giving to them - the children of Israel. Every place that the sole of your foot will tread upon I have given you, as I said to Moses. From the wilderness and this Lebanon as far as the great river, the river Euphrates, all the land of the Hittites, and to the Great Sea toward the going down of the sun, shall be your territory. No man shall be able to stand before you all the days of your life; as I was with Moses, so I will be with you. I will not leave you nor forsake you. Be strong and of good courage, for this people you shall divide as an inheritance the land, which I swore to their fathers to give them. Only be strong and very courageous, that you may observe to do according to all the law which Moses My servant commanded you; do not turn from it to the right hand or to the left, that you may prosper wherever you go. This book of the Law shall not depart from your mouth, but you shall meditate in it day and night, that you may observe to do according to all that is written in it. For then, you will make your way prosperous, and then you will have good success. Have I not commanded you? Be strong and of good courage, do not be afraid, nor be dismayed, for the Lord your God is with you wherever you go.

Joshua 1: 1 – 9, NKJV.

This was his purpose, vision, and dream given by God, to see Israel become a conquering nation of all the territory God had promised. The instruction he received from God was to keep His commandments, and to be strong in patience and courageous in faith, not becoming afraid or dismayed, and believe God is with you in whatever you do. This is also what he was telling Saul when he said, "And let it be, when these signs come to you, do as occasion demands, for God is with you." 1 Samuel 10: 7. As occasion demands – occasion demands a goal, a plan of strategy, a purpose for family, health, career, finances, recreation, without it someone else will plan it for you. We end up not fulfilling our potential. We end up helping him or her fulfill theirs and failing to fulfill our dreams. That is why Paul told us to redeem the time, because the days are evil, Have purpose in yourselves and good relations with others. see Ephesians 5: 16 and Mark 9: 50.

It's the same when a person is born again, "Therefore, if anyone is in Christ, he is a new creation *(another person)* old things *(old values)* have passed away, behold all things have become new *(new values)*. Now all things are of God....", 2 Corinthians 5: 17 – 18, NKJV, *(Emphasis Mine)*.

We too are to walk in courageous faith, being strong in patience as Joshua instructions exhorted Him. While we do God makes us over-comers and achievers in life leading us into triumph in all things in Christ. Knowing that in Christ means it is His will and done His way. Knowing that things are of God, who is working His purposes in all things for our good. We prove we believe it by committing ourselves to Him acknowledging His commandments in handling the affairs connected with our goals. He teaches what is important in life starting with living to bring Him glory through our dreams, relations with family, career pursuits, finances, and health. These areas are a divine call of stewardship, demanding goals setting to accomplish, fruitful lives for our children, wives, ourselves, along with contributing to welfare of the society we live in.

King David understood the walk of faith more than Saul did; we all know the story of David and Goliath. Neither David, nor Saul however, had any goals or strategy it seems to lead their children – no goals for the children's up bringing or education – I believe most do not. However, David did have faith, Saul had first dibs on Goliath but drew back along with all his men in fear, Saul's fear and indecisiveness was contagious and confusing to his soldiers. David saw him and had the spirit of decisiveness. I'll take him out was his attitude, and when he did all Israel took after the Philistines. His faith, courage, and decisiveness was inspiring and contagious.

Let's look at 1 Samuel 17: 41 – 47,

So the Philistine came, and began drawing near to David, and the man who bore the shield went before him. And when the Philistine looked about and saw David, he disdained him; for he was only a youth, ruddy and good looking. So the Philistine said to David, Am I a dog that you come to me with sticks?" And the Philistine cursed David by his gods. And the Philistine said to David, "Come to me, and I will give your flesh to the birds of the air and the beasts of the field!" Then David said to the Philistine, "You come to me with a sword, with a spear, and with a javelin, "But I come to you in the name of the Lord of hosts, the God of the Armies of Israel, whom you have defied. This day the Lord will deliver you into my hand, and I will strike you and take your head from you. And, this day I will give the carcasses of the camp of the Philistines to the birds of the air and the wild beasts of the earth, that all the earth may know that there is a God in Israel." Then all this assembly shall know that the Lord does not save with sword and spear; for the battle is the Lord's, and He will give you into our hands.

1 Samuel 17: 41 – 47, NKJV.

This was attitude – this is the positive attitude that God wants us to have in facing life, solving problems and accomplishing our goals. Paul manifested this kind of Spirit in Philippians, "I can do all things through Christ who strengthens me", Philippians 4: 13, NKJV. He does not want us to be like Saul who was sitting still while things worked out, just letting things happen. I believe goals and decisiveness please God when coupled with faith and prayer. Paul prayed for the Ephesians in chapter 3: 17, "... that Christ may dwell in your hearts by faith.... David had

God dwelling in his heart and boldly lived out his purpose. Solomon said, "The wicked flee when no one pursues, but the righteous are bold as a lion." Proverbs 28: 1, NKJV.

There is no problem or goal, you and God can not handle. Notice David did not say God what do I do. David was a decisive person in this instance with God dwelling in his heart by faith. This giant defies me; it defies the armies of Israel. So he took what was in his hand and worked with it and God did a miracle. See Exodus 4: 2 and 2 Kings 4: 2. God wants us to move forward in life and the next step will be revealed. You gain momentum with every step of forward motion – He makes your way prosper.

The words in this scripture remind me of the lyrics of a song "The Impossible Dream". You can find it on "You Tube" from various artist. Meditating on these words of this song illustrates the new mindset God wants to give to Christians, to be strong in patience and courageous in faith. They press on no matter what. They continue believing and using all things and circumstances to transform them into His image from glory to glory just as by the Spirit of the Lord (growing as a person and sowing seeds that provide a service to others). (See 2 Corinthians 3:18). They are gaining one victory and achievement after another, living life to the fullest, until the perfect day. The process is described in Proverbs 4: 18, and this song, I consider the legacy of one determined to fight the good fight of faith.

Those who know their God realize the words of these scriptures I have quoted, and lyrics of that old song have a lot in common. I hope it helps us realize the capacity of the person with faith, in God. Let us realize our God given potential, the faith and patience it takes to master that potential into skill, and the accomplishment of those goals they set proving faithful in their stewardship of this beautiful life. Let us discover the fulfillment of our potential through patience and encouragement of scripture, doing exploits with our life in the name of our God.

Some may say this song is not spiritual, remember Philippians 4: 8 and stay open-minded, look it up on "You Tube" and listen to it. Do not let Satan cause you to wear blinders. Jesus said "I will have mercy and not sacrifice." I had a man come to me once and tell me I shouldn't be teaching out of nothing but the King James version of the bible. I answered him, "Maybe this church isn't a fit for you." I'm still preaching out of the NKJV and the brother is still with us and doing a fine job in the church. So don't get so religious you can't learn something from the secular world that emulate the principles of God.

Doesn't Paul tell us to "Finally, my brethren, be strong *(patience)* in the Lord and *(have courageous faith)* in the power of His might." Ephesians 6: 10, NKJV. *(Emphasis Mine)*. Now here is a guy with the mind of the new life. Being strong in the Lord is expecting a way to be made with God's help – to confidently expect His help. This is the fruit of faith – the fruit of the Spirit – it is manifested in calm assurance, see Proverbs 28: 1 again.

Paul had purpose in life. It became his dream given from God, to preach the gospel throughout the known world and he followed through and was obedient to the heavenly calling and vision given him. He became a visionary for the gospel. His heavenly call, his vision is expressed in Romans, "Through Him and for his name sake, we have received grace and apostleship to call people from among the Gentiles to the obedience that comes from faith. And you also are among those who are called to belong to Jesus Christ." Romans 1: 5 - 6, NIV.

A person with the new life receives grace and knowledge to evolve and live with purpose to develop as a person in the image of Christ. Contributing back and attaining goals is part of that life. I say that because goals take discipline and the "New Life" is discipline. We use their gifts and talents to further the edification of Christ's bride, the church, relationships, and society. Those with the new life working in them are motivated to love, to give back through their gifts, and to work with integrity of purpose, for the glory of God, see 1 Peter 4: 10, "As each one has received a gift, minister it to one another, as good stewards of the manifold grace of God." They serve Christ by coming to the church with purpose, to serve in the body of Christ, to work and contribute to society with their talents, passions, visions, and goals to benefit all. They serve with the goal of service and producing fruit among all, intending to have influence for Christ sake, adorning His gospel. (See Titus 2: 9 – 10 & 1 Corinthians 9: 19 – 23 again).

They come home with the purpose of being a good spouse and parent for the glory of Christ and the edification of the family. They have goals for the family to fulfill their God given potentials. They go to work at their own business or as an employee with the purpose of being a team player, bringing their all to the table with all of their gifts and talents to glorify God. They have the philosophy of "Be there with all your heart." See Colossians 3: 23 – 25.

Experts say we only use 10 percent of our brains in our lifetime. In addition, the average person uses only 2 percent, I read somewhere once. If that is so, and I believe it is, you can train your brain by focusing on being productive and becoming above average. If that is true, why is it only two percent? I believe due to a lack of focus, the brain becomes dull through mental candy. Therefore life is dull, apathetic, and lethargic, instead of abundant and energetic as God intended, full of vitality.

I find it hard to believe that an apathetic brain could have energy, vitality, nor can be it have an extra happy life. If you have any of these mindsets and hate what you are and what you do, you have to change your attitude about what you do to ever change your environment to be happy. Here are the three steps in keeping that from happening to us.

"Establishing Your Goals"

Actually four - start with a better attitude is number one and the next three steps.

- You begin by asking yourself what and where you want to be and become this year, 5 years, ten years, and 20 – 30 years out.

- Write down your goals. If your goals aren't written, then they are wishes more than likely. Start with a daily planner. Write all your goals on the inside of the cover where you can review them, several times a day. This helps get your goals into your subconscious mind. When opportunity arises to help you move forward, the subconscious mind will alert you. God made our brains that way.

- Next, chart a course, a strategy, for your goals breaking them down into smaller goals to make big goals easier. "How do you eat an elephant, one bite at a time" as the old Indian proverb goes? I advocate several goals as a must. They are as follows: Spiritual, Family, Health, Financial, Career, Relationship, and Recreation.

You begin by asking yourself the question as to what you want in each of these areas and then plan for them starting with how you see it as though you all ready have it. Then build your strategy, building it and adjusting daily, weekly, monthly, yearly and out to five years and beyond with a plan to bring all your goals to pass.

The next part of maturing in this the "New Life" is setting goals to leave an honorable legacy. Now that you have put on the new man (life in Christ) let us, go on to maturity.

CHAPTER VIII

"MATURING IN THE NEW LIFE"

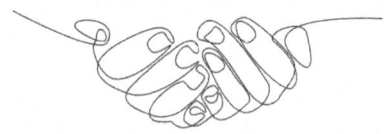

What is maturity? When you began growing in the new life, learning to the apply the personality habits of the Spirit and giving back service to God and others. We also begin to set goals in life to fulfill our purpose. We are well on our way of succeeding, having a fruitful and an abundant life for God's glory. Hebrews challenges us this way:

For though by this time you ought to be teachers, you need someone to teach you again the first principles of the oracles of God, and you have come to need milk and not solid food. For everyone who partakes only of milk is unskilled in the word of righteousness, for he is a babe. But solid food belongs to those who are of full age, that is, those who by reason of use have their senses exercised to discern both good and evil. Therefore, leaving the discussion of the elementary principles of Christ, let us go on to perfection, not laying again the foundation of repentance from dead works and of faith toward God, of the doctrine of baptisms, of laying on of hands, of resurrection of the dead, and eternal judgment. And this we will do if God permits.

Hebrews 5: 12 – Hebrews 6: 1 – 3.

We are all evolving continually. You are either making progress or regressing. When you hit a plateau, hang on. Paul, an expert on the new life wrote, "Not that I have already attained, or am already perfected, but I press on, that I may lay hold of that for which Christ Jesus has also laid hold of me." Philippians 3: 12, NKJV. We are to keep moving forward through meditation; prayer, pursuing love, patience, faith, and becoming productive and contributing stewards of God's grace and His resources are availed to us through His lovingkindness and providence. The best way is to have a mindset of goal setting and working smart. By working smart I mean using good time management principles.

Some in Christian circles would say this is worldly, but I say the enemy came to steal, kill, and destroy your God given potential and definitely your time. He does this through teaching us self-destructive habits and negative thinking, as such that comes from the naysayers of life that come against our accomplishments.

Proverbs says, "He who tills his land will be satisfied with bread, but he who follows frivolity is devoid of understanding", Proverbs 12: 11, NKJV. We are not to waste the resources God has given us. Time and the mind are the biggest resources God has given us. Using it wisely within the parameters of Gods' wisdom, we inherit health, wealth, and everything positive to nurture an abundant life. "See then that you walk circumspectly, not as fools but as wise, redeeming the time, because the days are evil." Ephesians 5: 15 – 16, NKJV.

Some understand this after we receive and begin to grow in the grace and knowledge that is in Jesus Christ. Some believe God has got to inspire everything. David said God doesn't have a house to live in once, that was his idea, and God said it was a good one. He also told Him who would build it. Some have a tendency to wait on God to move them toward everything, and God is saying get in the game of life and live it - without leaving Him out. Set some goals for your self, for your family, your health, finances, career, etc. and go for it for, God is with you, see 1 Samuel 10: 6 -7 again. When David told the prophet Nathan, I got an idea, I'm going to build God a House, the prophet replied, "Then Nathan said to the king, "Go do all that is in your heart for God is with you." 2 Samuel 7:3, NKJV. God didn't chide David for being a visionary. David was a visionary leader all of his life. We limit God when we put limits on ourselves. God wants you live life abundantly. An abundant life is full of satisfying achievements. It isn't give your money and God will make you rich for it – it's give me an opportunity and by God's grace I'll achieve exploits in His name will give me an abundant life.

Jesus taught it this way, "He also said to His disciples: "There was a certain rich man who had a steward, and an accusation was brought to him that this man was wasting his goods *(time, grace, and resources are His goods, let us use them in faithfulness)*. So he called him and said to him. "What is this I hear about you? Give an account of your stewardship, for you can no longer be steward. ".... He who is faithful in what is least is faithful also in much, and he who is unjust in what is least is unjust also in much. Therefore if you have not been faithful in the unrighteous mammon, who will commit to your trust the true riches." Luke 16: 1 – 11, NKJV, *(Emphasis Mine) (Read all eleven verses)*. Time is unrighteous mammon- eternity is the true riches. Potential is grace given at birth and it is meant to be used up in this life to the fullest. "As each one has received a gift, minister it to one another as good stewards of the manifold grace of God", 1 Peter 4: 10, NKJV. Gifts have to be developed, don't limit God develop them and give back to His glory! I do believe in sowing and reaping, and he who gives sparingly will reap sparingly. Give of yourself bountifully to be more and then you will be bountifully more to be more to them you minister too. When you are more and give it away in service to others, you add value to their life, thus making others rich. Remember the one talent man who hid his talent and didn't develop it, His master was displeased that he sit on it and didn't develop it. We should realize that the Lord is the master in that parable and He is encouraging us not to limit Him in our personal development, to be more for His glory.

Jesus did not say life would be easy, but He promised to be with us and to keep us. Once you are dealing with the sinful habits of the flesh, God wants to take you to to the next level in the new life that we are learning about through His grace. The best way to deal with sin is get your mind on some good healthy goals to occupy your mind. He wants your life to be productive, spiritually and socially fruitful so you can experience a productive ambitious life, influencing souls for the kingdom. Glorifying His work in you as His masterpiece work. Read Ephesians 2: 10 NKJV and 2 Thessalonians 1: 11 – 12 NIV. This is living the abundant life.

First Jesus said, "The thief comes only to steal and kill and destroy, I have come that they may have life, and have it to the full." John 10: 10, NIV. The thief steals the abundant life by getting us to buy into the wisdom of folly, and sin, in contrast to the wisdom of God that tells us to rule our lives diligently. This contrast is asserted to especially in the book of Proverbs. Jesus is teaching, if you follow My wisdom you will find an abundance of life both now and forever. The wisdom of this new life teaches us to be industrious. Some seem to teach we can barter with God through our offerings to get something from Him without applying ourselves to due diligence. The way offerings are taught by some would give you the impression that God is running a lottery. And God does bless for giving to His purposes, but I believe we need discernment in giving also.

The hand of the diligent will rule *(Be the Head not the Tail)*, but the lazy man will be put to forced labor.

Proverbs 12: 24, NKJV *(Emphasis Mine)*.

The scripture can't be broken, let's get diligent with our life and stop playing someones lottery. Diligence and excellence glorify God. Secondly, Jesus said in Matthew 12: 30, "He who is not with Me is against Me, and he who does not gather with Me scatters abroad", Matthew 2: 30, NKJV. Proverbs expresses this wisdom taught in these scriptures this way, "The fruit of the righteous is a tree of life, and he who wins souls is wise." Proverbs 11; 30, NKJV. Jesus and Solomon are saying if we walk in the wisdom of God – we will influence others for Christ when they see your good works they will glorify God in you. Matthew affirms it, "Let your light so shine before men that they may see your good works and glorify your Father in heaven." Matthew 5: 16, NKJV. Light stands for understanding or wisdom in the bible. In addition, goals are the best way of showing what God can do for a committed life to His values and goals that contribute to your personal development and the welfare of others.

Paul expressed the effect of walking in God's wisdom this way, "Now thanks be to God who always leads us in triumph in Christ, and through us diffuses the fragrance of His knowledge to every place. For we are to God the fragrance of Christ among those who are being saved and among those who are perishing. To the one, we are the aroma of death leading to death, and to the other, the aroma of life leading to life. And who is sufficient for these things?" 2 Corinthians 2: 14 – 16, NKJV. What has He made us sufficient to be fellow laborers with God? Walking in His revealed truth and wisdom toward others, see Colossians 4: 5, below. "For we are God's fellow workers; you are God field, you are God's building. According to the grace of God, which was given me, as a wise master builder, I have laid the foundation, and another builds on it. But let each one take heed how he builds on it." 1 Corinthians 3: 9 – 10. We bring conviction if we live consistently by the core values taught in God's word. That is why Paul exhorted us to redeem the time to walk as wise and not fools as expressed above in Ephesians 5: 17. Paul said the same thing to the Colossians but in different words, "Walk in wisdom toward those who are outside, redeeming the time. Let your speech always be with grace, seasoned with salt *(purpose or conviction)* that you may know how you ought to answer each one.", Colossians 4: 5 –6, NKJV, *(Emphasis Mine)*.

When Jesus said that you might have life and that life more abundantly. It comes through consistently living after His principles, purpose, and having goals consistent with our inner most passions and pursuing them with diligence, purpose, and conviction. Our goals help us to be fruitful and productive in the world in a good way. Our trials from our goals stretch us giving meaning to life and make us more emotionally whole over time – this is the abundant life in this world. Proverbs expresses it like this, "A sound heart is life to the body, but envy is rottenness to the bones.", Proverbs 14: 30, NKJV. Soundness of heart is wholeness of emotion, body, and spirit it comes through living after good core values and accomplishments that builds self-esteem and self-confidence. Proverbs also says it, "A desire accomplished is sweet to the soul, but it is an abomination to fools to depart from evil." Proverbs 13: 19, NKJV. As I tell youth, "Drifting without Purpose is a Vice." An unprofitable servant is aimless or one who starts something and does not finish what they start due to a negative mindset of excuses and apathetic aimlessness of purpose. If we chart out a course and stay committed to it until we accomplish them we learn endurance and self confidence. God is glorified by our our lives and in the accomplishments of the goals He has given us, if accomplished according to His principles gleaned from in His wisdom.

As a matter of fact 1 Corinthians 7: 24 says, "Brethren, let each one remain with God in that state in which he was called." Read the whole section of scripture, verses 16 - 24. Paul is telling them to bloom where you are through contentment of patience and diligently laboring with purpose, see Mark 9: 50 again. However, if you read the passage, Verse 21, it tells us, "Were you called a slave *(employee)*? Do not be concerned about it; but if you can be made free, rather use it (See Verse 21, *(Emphasis Mine)*." Change careers follow your own aspiration or, "Bloom Where You Are". Unless you can be freed up and do something else you love that sows good seeds toward others and grows you toward your potential, grow where you are.

The brain and mind are so vast that you will never accomplish everything you are capable of doing. There just is not enough time in this age to learn it all; but we can always be a learner until death, attempting to connect all those neuron connections.

God gave Joshua a purpose along with the whole nation of Israel, but we find in Judges chapter 2: 1 – 10 that they failed to have the commitment to fulfill their destiny and died grieving with regret, see also Psalm 78: 32 - 33. We do not want that to happen to us. When you die you will still have brain left that you did not use up, imagine that, "Use it or Lose It", even though you are going to lose some of it anyway, use as much as possible now. Isn't that laughable - funny when you think about it – you will still have capacity to learn and create new things with your mind when you die, it want be used up – awesome – you can't use it up! Thomas Edison said, "If we did all the things we were capable of doing, we'd literally astound ourselves."

We are creatures of learning and growth. Become involved were you work by taking on more responsibility and learning new things. Were you worship, volunteer, and pray for the services, the Pastor, and families in the church. Get involved with your community to give back something. Christians ought to be the biggest givers of themselves at work, community, and church or find something that fulfills and completes them that they can give too. You can do a great job, if the work you do is boring and meaningless to you, pray for direction but until something new opens reframe your thinking to give whatever you do - your best!

Paul said, "Command them do good, that they be rich in good deeds, and to be generous and willing to share." 1 Timothy 6: 18, NIV. To become productive in life and be happy and whole, you have to follow God's principles of becoming more through due diligence following your vision or dream that is important to you. When that dream fulfills a ministry or sows good seed that benefits the human race, it gives glory to God and honors you - give it your whole heart. God does not want us to drift along aimlessly. Drifting through life is a vice. Proverbs says, "Wisdom is in the sight of him who has understanding, but the eyes of a fool are on the ends of the earth", Proverbs 17: 24, NKJV. Proverbs says again, "Where there is no vision, the people perish *(due to aimlessness)*. But he that keepeth the law, *(of diligence)*, happy is he", Proverbs 29: 18, KJV, *(Emphasis Mine)*. If we keep his word we will have purpose, purpose develops self-discipline, endurance, and more purpose. Doesn't his word tell us to be purposeful, see Mark 9: 50 again. Most beleaguer sexual sins, stealing, lying, violence and neglect the teaching on diligence. Diligence is part of the gospel.

If we move, out in faith and commitment, God moves things into our life just at the right time to move us forward. Dreaming is the beginning of vision and goal setting is the initial step to the commitment of something grand. We begin the momentum by goal setting and faith. Then God supplies the resources. God is faithful to direct our steps and show the next step. Purpose gives us something else to live for and purpose adds vitality and energy to our life. Having goals are a part of faithful stewardship. "Matthew says it this way,

For the kingdom of heaven is like a man traveling to a far country, who called his own servants and delivered his goods to them. And to one he gave five talents, to another two, and to another one, to each according to his own ability; and immediately he went on a journey. Then he who received the five talents went and traded with them, and made another five talents. And likewise, he who had received two gained two more also. But, he who had received one went and dug in the ground, and hid his lord's money. After a long time the lord of those servants came and settled accounts with them. So he who had received five talents came and brought five other talents, saying, Lord, you delivered to me five talents; look, I have gained five more talents besides them." His Lord said to him, "Well done, good and faithful servant; you were faithful over a few things, I will make you ruler over many things. Enter into the joy of your Lord. He who had received two talents came and said," Lord you delivered to me two talents; look, I have gained two more talents besides them." His Lord said to him, "Well done, good and faithful servant; you have been faithful over a few things, I will make you ruler over many things. Enter into the joy of your Lord. Then he who had received the one talent came and said, "Lord, I knew you to be a hard man, reaping where you have not sown, and gathering where you have not scattered seed. And I was afraid, and went and hid your talent in the ground. Look, there you have what is yours. But his lord answered and said to him, "You wicked and lazy servant, you knew that I reap where I have not sown, and gather where I have not scattered seed. So you ought to have deposited my money with the bankers, and at my coming I would have received back my own with interest. Therefore, take the talent from him, and give it to him who has ten talents. For to everyone who has, more will be given, and he will have abundance; but from him who does not have, even what he has will be taken away. And cast the unprofitable servant in the outer darkness. There will be weeping and gnashing of teeth.

Matthew 25: 14 – 30, NKJV.

God has given all of us abilities with the potential to be productive. He wants us to develop and use them to contribute good in life that contributes to the welfare of the kingdom and society that our conduct might honor Him. When we are afraid or just do not try for whatever reasons, we fail God. I heard a statement made by one of the characters co-starring on "The Waltons" once say; "You are what your limitations make you." Each of us have limitations to overcome, be it education, money issues, or just plane negative mindedness; they are not to hold us back. We are to let our goals and dreams stretch us. By solving the issues accompanied with goals, overcoming them builds our character and confidence in God and ourselves. If we will choose following through on a dream, making it our vision, purpose, and serve God with salt, God will do His part as we exercise the maturity of faith and commitment to see it accomplished.

The book of Proverbs teaches the principles of God by contrasting God's wisdom with the wisdom of folly. Proverbs, "Where there is no revelation, the people cast off restraint *(self-discipline to do due diligence)*; but happy is he who keeps the law." Proverbs 29: 18, NKJV, *(Emphasis Mine)*. Without purposeful living, people feed on mental candy in excess and perish or disappear with the status quo because of aimlessness. They play now and pay later, whereas God's word teaches pay now and play later, see Proverbs 12: 24 and 27: 23 – 27. God will direct the path and supply the resources of those who supply the commitment, diligently seeking good, seeking to be faithful stewards of the manifold grace of God, see 1 Peter 4: 10 - 11.

Peter Quoted David saying in Psalm 34: 12 – 16. "For "He who would love life and see good days, let him refrain his tongue from evil, and his lips from speaking deceit. Let him turn away from evil and do good, let him seek peace and pursue it. For the eyes of the Lord are on the righteous, and His ears are open to their prayers; but the face of the Lord is against those who do evil." 1 Peter 3: 10 –12, NKJV, also see James 1: 26 - 27.

Moments of epiphany and revelation show plainly the next step that just comes when needed. Proverbs puts it this way also, "But the path of the just is like the shining sun, that shines ever brighter unto the perfect day. The way of the wicked is like darkness; they do not know what makes them stumble." Proverbs 4: 18 – 19, NKJV. I emphatically believe the honor of God has to be first in all decisions. Then if we are committed to the purpose we can be sure of, the next step and resources will surely be revealed to you in the accomplishment of your purpose until your purpose is established.

With this in mind, we constantly pray for you, that our God may count you worthy of his calling, and that by his power he may fulfill every good purpose of yours and every act prompted by your faith. We pray this so that the name of our Lord Jesus may be glorified in you, and you in him, according to the grace of our God and the Lord Jesus Christ.

2 Thessalonians 1: 11 – 12, NIV.

Proverbs says, "Commit your works to the Lord, and your thoughts will be established.", Proverbs 16: 3, NKJV. God gave David a goal, a purpose to shepherd the nation of Israel and God established it, See 2 Samuel 5: 12. David, however, had to move forward in life as the doors opened, even though his enemy continually was trying to track him down to kill him. At the right time God delivered David and gave him partial possession of the kingdom in that He made him king over Judah. All the time before this David lived each day building on his future in faithfulness to God and waiting on God to show the next step until the perfect day that he was established king over all Israel, see 2 Samuel 5: 12.

God was doing the leading and keeping His hand on David. David just had a promise that caused him at times to ponder about his destiny. Your dream is the promise of what your future. It can be established if you pursue your dream on a daily basis and put your life and efforts in Gods' care, See 2 Timothy 1: 12.

I am not so sure that David understood vision and purpose as well as his son Solomon did in Proverbs 29: 18. It was another seven years before God made him king over all Israel, 2 Samuel 5: 12. Why it took another seven years for David to inherit the entire Kingdom is a mystery, but to be sure, it kept David humble. Lord John Acton said, "Power tends to corrupt - absolute power corrupts absolutely. Great men are almost always bad men." Could it be God had this in mind when He groomed David as the Shepherd over all Israel to spare him this temptation? Even still he failed morally with Bathsheba as did Solomon fail over a desire for women. It seems to have validated what Abraham Lincoln said about power, "Nearly all men can stand adversity, but if you want to test a man's character, give him power."

The only way I believe to avoid these pit falls is to make your purpose to grow toward your full potential and to conform into His image continually. Is not this what Jesus was alluding to in the parable of the ten virgins in Matthew 25: 1 – 13, Watch He told them. Five were wise and served God with purpose and five were foolish, apathetic therefore reckless and thus aimless. Abraham Lincoln said it this way "I do not think much of a man who is not wiser today than he was yesterday." Wiser today means watchful not to loosing ground by recklessness and aimlessness - by indiscretions and mistakes. And, isn't this what Epaphras prayed for the Colossians, "Epaphras, who is one of you, a bondservant of Christ, greets you, always laboring fervently for you in prayers, that you may stand perfect and complete in all the will of God. For I bear him witness that he has a great zeal for you, and those who are in Laodicea, and those in Hierapolis." In praying for these to be perfect and complete in all the will of God, Colossians 4: 12, NKJV. Was he not praying for their personal growth and maturity in all things? Of course he was!

How was David different from Saul, David was quick to repent, Saul's religion was superficial, he performed religious pious acts for show. When Samuel confronted Saul, he made excuses; the people made me do it, see 1 Samuel 15: 24 – 30. It is always grievous to see promising individuals fall. Power can cause us to drop our guard and become high-minded. This will lead us to become self centered, reckless, and aimlessly irresponsible with our time. David, Saul and the exhortation of scripture should teach us to guard life with prayer. David wrote prayers in the psalms, Saul evidently entertained himself with thoughts of grandeur. See 1 Samuel 15: 12. "Continue earnestly in prayer, being vigilant in it with thanksgiving." Colossians 4: 2, NKJV. Handle life with prayer.

However, those who fall we should concentrate more on confronting with the purpose of restoring and giving people a chance to begin afresh as we discussed in another chapter. Failure has to give a person a new perspective as it did for David.

Saul never seemed to have the conviction that showed he had a new perspective when confronted. David on the other hand was quick to repent, get a new perspective, and keep living for God's purposes - personal growth in character and achievement. Did he not keep working toward supplying materials for the building of the temple, that diligence was part of his legacy in his old age.

Proverbs teaches diligence it does not praise slothfulness, it condemns sloth and aimlessness. Part of a person being happy is working hard toward a goal that is fulfilling to them, provides glory to God, and provides a service for others. To be a happy person we need to have a worthwhile purpose – giving back something in service to others and the kingdom of God. David knew he was a soldier and a commander by God's design and was called to be a warrior king and worked faithfully at it everyday. His pathway was like a shining light that shined brighter unto the perfect day of opportunity when God gave advancement. David and our life reach a tipping point if we stay with it long enough, believing and waiting on the faithfulness of God that takes us over the top.

Your dream, if it benefits others, glorifies God, and gives you satisfaction, do it – for God is with you! Accomplishment of purpose or the benchmarks related to that purpose fills the mind and the spirit with, self-esteem, self confidence, and faith in God after each benchmark of accomplishment. Progress fuels your spirit with enthusiasm; it adds vitality, energy, confidence, and self-esteem, for the next phase of your goal. It is part of your development process of growing in the new life and becoming a person of wholeness manifesting the abundant life. All the fuel you get from accomplishment such as new energy, vitality, and stronger faith in God and yourself ought to make you live purposely, no matter how hard the road might be - it will be worth it!

God is involved in every part of our development for our good. He allows our goals to stretch us to our potential and grow us spiritually while He keeps us, creating the image of His Son in us throw them, see 1 Peter 4: 19.

Faith pleases God and without faith, it is impossible to please God. The book of Romans 1: 17, say that the righteousness of God is revealed from faith to faith. We accept the grace of God by faith, and from that time, we walk by faith and through faith, we realize the purposes God has for us because He is directing our steps. (Read 2 Corinthians 5: 17 - 18 and Proverbs 3: 5 - 6 again). We purpose to repent and change our behavior and that includes not living aimlessly – it is a sin. It is slothful stewardship and that is sin. The opposite of diligence is slothfulness and that is caused chiefly by aimlessness. Someone said if you don't know where you are going, any road will get you there. Proverbs advocates due diligence in every area of life. Having faith causes us to have purpose in ourselves and live out our dreams with more passion because of our faith. Knowing that we are not alone and knowing we are created for purpose. God does not do things recklessly or disorderly – look how organized the human body and the universe is. You came into this world just on time and will leave on His time schedule. During that time, we fight the good fight of faith pursuing purity, and godliness, and purpose, filled with passion for living to His glory. Your tombstone has a birth day – death date. What we do with the years the dash represents is up to us.

Jesus said, "Salt is good, but if the salt loses its flavor *(Commitment to taste)*, how will you season it? Have salt *(purpose)* in yourselves, and have peace with one another." Mark 9: 50, NKJV. To be purposeful in a good thing is healthy. Being purposeful to live by God's principles and values is the first and highest purpose. Then the dreams of accomplishment that contribute that are in our Spirit are next. It gives the mind something to focus on besides folly. "Where there is no revelation (vision/goals) the people cast off restraint *(self-discipline)*; but happy is he who keeps the law." Proverbs 29: 18, NKJV, *(Emphasis Mine)*.

When a person has a passion for a good thing, it pleases God. "He who earnestly *(Passionately or Zealously)* seeks good finds favor. But trouble will come to him who seeks evil." Proverbs 11: 27, NKJV, *(Emphasis Mine)*. Idleness breeds a lack of restraint and lack of restraint breeds evil. The old adage, "An idle mind is the devil's play ground", can be applied to this verse because, "Aimlessness is a Vice", per James Allen. It is always good to be diligent *(passionate)* in a good thing. Your life is to be productive and glorifying to God – it can not happen without passion and God's blessing as it should. Pursuing a good purpose to fulfill a dream of what you would like to do with your life has to come from passion and confidence or you will be double minded about it.

"Let him who stole steal no longer, but rather let him labor, working with his hands what is good, that he may have something to give him who has need." Ephesians 4: 28, NKJV. We are to contribute, bring something to the table in life. If it is honest, it is good, if it meets a need for your fellowman, it is good. Those that design cars, computers, telephones, etc. are all making life better and more comfortable for us all. It also provides a good living for their families while they have fun doing what they love to do. If your present vocation is fulfilling, you are probably giving it your heartfelt best. If not, you should be pursuing a purpose, you can give yourself to wholeheartedly. Paul contended that "And whatever you do, do it heartily, as to the Lord and not to men, knowing that from the Lord you will receive the reward of inheritance; for you serve the Lord." Colossians 3: 23 – 24, NKJV. Pursue excellence in whatever you do and you will have to excel. Proverbs claims, "Do you see a man who excels in his work? He will stand before kings; He will not stand before unknown men." Proverbs 22: 29, NKJV. Get good at what you do, by becoming more excellent at what you do and you will be more valuable. Your value will make room for you with leaders of men.

Solomon put this perspective on it, "The hand of the diligent *(purposeful)* will rule, but the lazy *(aimless)* man will be put to forced labor." Proverbs 12: 24, NKJV, *(Emphasis Mine)*. If you don't set goals for yourself, you will work for someone who did. Verse 27 says, "The lazy man does not roast what he took in hunting, but diligence (responsible purpose) is man's precious possession." Proverbs 2: 27, NKJV, (Emphasis Mine). Due diligence is man's precious possession. Due diligence and purpose shows in how a man takes care of his property, how he manages his potential, and each opportunity for progress, how he feeds his mind as well. You also have to be diligent about your dream. Your dream or job is also property and those who are diligent, will eventually; be known as the visionaries of this world, the shakers and movers on their job, in their career field, or industry. Their life will have had significance when they pass.

So get up and get started, pursue your unreachable star and stay the course until you attain the unreachable. Those who do are remembered forever. The dreamers that do not follow through on their purpose in life are not known, but people who do contribute are.

CHAPTER IX

"ACCOMPLISHMENT OF LIFE'S PURPOSES TAKES FOCUS"

"He that tills his land will be satisfied with bread. But he who follows frivolity *(Mental Candy)* is devoid of understanding *(Ain't too Bright)*." Proverbs 12: 11, NKJV, *(Emphasis Mine)*.

Let me paraphrase this for our time, "He that focusses on his purposes and sets and focusses on his goals will be fed, but he who lives aimlessly is devoid of understanding." He that has focus will prosper in what he focuses on.

Focus is like using a magnifying glass to start a fire. As the sunlight focuses through the magnifying glass on the matter in hand, it begins to smolder and then a flame ignites and consumes the material. It is the same way with the project phases of accomplishing a goal. As you focus singled mindedly on each phase of a goal and continue working away at it until the objective is reached with excellence, it evolves into achievement. It gives satisfaction contributing to the wholeness of a person's soul, especially when completed with excellence.

There is a saying I think of when I get in a rush, "If you don't have time to do it right the first time – How is it you have time to it right the second time?" Excellence glorifies God in what we do and honors us. That doesn't mean I claim to be good at what I do. I see everything has a learning curve. I give my best and I see my skill getting better and that satisfies me. What we are looking for is progress and excellence, not perfection.

Our first focus should first be our walk with Christ, per Ephesians 5: 14 - 17, "Therefore He says, "Awake you who sleep, Arise from the dead, and Christ will give you light." See then that you walk circumspectly *(purposely not aimlessly)*, not as fools but as wise, redeeming the time, because the days are evil. Therefore do not be unwise, but understand what the will of the Lord is." Ephesians 5: 14 – 17, NKJV, *(Emphasis Mine)*. Stay focussed on what matters – "Seek you first the kingdom of God and all these things will be added to you." Matthew 6: 33, NKJV. Learn something new everyday to make progress toward your full potential as a person of character and skill.

God is concerned about your purposes, I believe He put them there at birth and some we realize as we get older and progress in life. It is the thing that fulfills you and gives you good morale. "As for every man to whom God has given riches and wealth and given him power to eat of it, to receive his heritage and rejoice in his labor - this is a gift of God. For he will not dwell unduly on the days of his life, because God keeps him busy with the joy *(Passions, Goals and Purposes)* of his heart." Ecclesiastes 5: 19 –20, NKJV, *(Emphasis Mine)*. The joy of his heart is God's gift fulfilling a meaningful purpose in this life to God's glory. He is purposely living because he knows aimlessness is a vice, thus God rewards him for commitment to Him and good stewardship of his time. He gets to enjoy it because in pursuing his purpose he honors God first, (See Proverbs 3: 9 – 10 and Malachi 3: 10.

God considers faithfulness in using our time for some good that benefits others, pursuing excellence in what we do, worshipping Him with the first fruits of our income, family rearing to produce godly seed, a godly business, or profession as faithfulness to Him. Faithfulness to God causes us to grow in more knowledge of God and in His grace.

Listen to what is said about revelation in the book of 1 Samuel, "Now the boy Samuel ministered to the Lord before Eli. And the word of the Lord was rare in those days: there was no widespread revelation." 1 Samuel 3: 1, NKJV. Revelation is one of the ways God manifests Himself and His will to us. "He who has My commandments and keeps them, it is he who loves Me. And he who loves Me will be loved by My Father, and I will love him and manifest Myself to him." John 14: 21, NKJV. God will teach His character and the direction our life is to take to us if we put him first in all things. The next step becomes plain if we keep moving forward and learning these things. Deuteronomy says, "And you will remember the Lord your God, for it is He who gives you power to get wealth, that He may establish His covenant which He swore to your fathers, as it is this day." Deuteronomy 8: 18, NKJV. Let us not think anything is of ourself because God will not give His glory to another. "Instead you ought to say, "If the Lords wills, we shall live and do this or that." But now you boast in your arrogance. All such boasting is evil. Therefore, to him who knows to do good and does not do it, to him it is sin." James 4: 15 – 17, NKJV.

The rule in life is to keep moving forward in faith. Our muscles teach us that - use it or lose it. Psalm says, "Oh how great is Your goodness, which you have laid up for those who fear You, which you have prepared for those who trust in You in the presence of the sons of men!" Psalm 31: 19, NKJV.

I emphasize God first because I believe that if we put God first, everything we put our hands to in our spiritual and secular affairs will prosper too. John believed it and asserts to this in 3 John "Beloved, I pray that you may prosper in all things and be in health, just as your soul prospers." 3 John 2, NKJV. As you make progress in personal growth, and spiritual growth, spiritual growth is part of personal growth, along with the development of our gifts and talents, God prospers your efforts toward success if you honor Him in all you do.

I was doing some yard work this week, cutting down some holly bushes. I had cloth gloves on and a yard rake and I was using the yard rake like a shovel. I could not touch the leaves due to the points going through the glove. I pushed the clippings into the garbage can using the rake portion of the rake. As I was getting to the end though I wondered how am I going to get the residue up. As I continued it occurred to me, I could use the trash can as a back drop and get the final clippings up on the rake and into the container. I had to pick a few little pieces up but not enough to mention. Receiving the next revelation of how is like that, you do what you know you can do and the understanding for the next step will come to you at the right time.

It is the same in spiritually at times, other times it takes prayer, and sometimes fasting. Light or understanding, will be given at the right time when we ask for it. "If any of you lacks wisdom, let him ask of God, who gives to all liberally and without reproach, and it will be given to him. But, let him ask in faith with no doubting, for he who doubts is like a wave of the sea driven and tossed by the wind. For let not that man suppose that he will receive anything from the Lord; he is a double minded man, unstable in all his ways." James 1: 5 – 8, NKJV.

However, a man without a purpose lacks understanding of where he is going. He has no destination in life, and if we aim at nothing that is what we will get most of the time. Remember "Drifting With Out Purpose is a Vice", and "Were there is no revelation the people perish" and I want to add, perish without ever making a difference. If you never aim at anything - you never hit anything. A jack of all trades doesn't major in anything. Therefore he is isn't very valuable. He might be a good person, a good family man, but he doesn't bring a lot of value to the table in the market place. Choose your passion and major in it.

Has God given you a revelation or a knowing of your place in the body of Christ. Has He given you a dream of accomplishing something in life for His glory and your satisfaction? Are you pursuing it? Do you have a vision statement for your life? How about a purpose statement and a daily itinerary, a daily schedule made out for the next day to aim at what you want to accomplish by the end of the day? These things keep you focussed on that day and every other day until the perfect day of accomplishment. The big picture that you feel God is calling or allowing you to accomplish is what focus will contribute to your life. If you do, you will accomplish more than the average person that is drifting through each day.

Romans 12: 3 – 8, puts the perspective on focus this way, "For I say, through the grace given to me, to everyone who is among you, not to think of himself more highly than he ought to think, but to think soberly, as God has dealt to each one a measure of faith. For as we have many members in one body, but all the members do not have the same function, so we, being many, are one body in Christ, and individually members of one another. Having then gifts differing according to the grace that is given to us, let us use them if prophecy, let us prophesy in proportion to our faith *(assurance of purpose)*; or ministry, let us use *(focus on)* it in our ministering; he who teaches, in teaching, he who exhorts, in exhortation; he who gives, with liberality, he who leads, with diligence (of purpose); he who shows mercy, with cheerfulness." Romans 12: 3 – 8, NKJV, *(Emphasis Mine)*.

As we begin doing tasks that we have never done before, there will be a learning curve. However, as you push forward with forward motion the next step just appears by way of "A-Ha!" moments from the subconscious or a direct word from the

Holy Spirit. Like the raking of the Holly clippings, I mentioned earlier. It is the same with every endeavor in our lives. Using the bag came from the subconscious mind that stores up recall for use at the right time. Sometimes we may realize we need more training in an area to become skilled at some purpose we want to succeed at.

Although, we receive a word from the Holy Spirit that confirms us to the ministry and in directions in other matters. Focussing on what we do and what we want to accomplish as with the clippings gave me the next step from the subconscious without even thinking heavily about it. Actually, it is the same to some extent in ministry. Sometimes opportunity and events just unfold but I believe all comes from God and you know what to do because you have prepared. As Abraham Lincoln stated, "I will prepare and someday my chance will come." At other times, you have to discern what is the next step prayerfully, see James 1: 5 – 8 again.

When we focus on every area of our life. Spiritually, there are times we need to separate ourselves daily to prayer, meditation, and the study of the word of God. After prayer and meditation my whole mental outlook and disposition is changed. Prayer and meditation in His word, with focus on spiritual, personal, and career development is the main part of the infrastructure of life. The changes that takes place on the inner man or the inner self are discussed in Romans chapter six through chapter eight for spiritual growth. Through spiritual growth, evolves the rest of the new man. I believe this should be the main infrastructure of everyone's life. We should be thanking God for His forgiveness and focussing and meditating on the things of the spirit. We exchange the thought life of the natural man for that of the spiritual man. We learn what we are to meditate on in the scriptures. Making these principles and values that are to be the focus and foundation of our thought life that we may discern the moments to apply them rightly. If we do this I know God will be with us to give us peace in all that we do, see Philippians 4: 8 - 9.

The most important parts of my life are God, family, country, health, career, and finances. The scriptures have a lot to say about family.

First, the new life teaches us that pleasing God is our first focus.

Secondly, as we focus on what the faith says about our families, wives, children, and our parents, it gives assurance we are to nurture our relationships with them, in pursuit of their welfare while they are with us.

Third part of the infrastructure of my life is my country, being the citizen I am supposed to be. To obey the laws of the land, pray for and respect the officials over me, and pay the taxes I owe.

Fourth is my health, developing nutritional eating habits, exercising for fitness, and staying up to date on the subject of health. These are necessary to have a better quality of life so I can enjoy it without being sick or diseased.

Fifth is my career. After retiring from the military in 1989, my occupational career has been mainly a bi-vocational pastor for the past eight years. Serta Mattress is where I compensated my income while pastoring Grace Assembly of God until the church was out of debt. Nevertheless, when I was able, in accordance with 1 Corinthians 7: 21. I went full time pastoring when I retired from there at age 62.

Sixth is my finances learning to invest in assets instead of creating debt that has no ROI (Return on Investment) involved. This usually requires someone that is a professional in that area, but a savings account and IRA is a good place to start. Alternatively, the competence for using a skill you like to do to create a living. The stock market or other investments are for people with purpose; the lottery and trinkets are for people who live on luck being reckless and aimless hoping they will be lucky. The stock market and real estate is a better bet. I believe in the blessing of God on effort of purpose. More people get rich on purpose than on luck. Abraham Lincoln asserted, "All things come to him who waits, but only those things left behind by those who hustle." All of these areas require focus, if you are going to grow and finally attain results in these areas.

Focus requires us also to set goals and measurable benchmarks to our chosen destination. Measurable benchmarks are small goals contained in your strategy related to the overall goal and measures progress. There are times when God is leading and we do not know the destination. As with Abraham's calling, "By faith Abraham obeyed when he was called to go out to the place which he would receive as an inheritance. And he went out not knowing where he was going." Hebrews 11: 8. We go into those places of life and our goal should be to make it better and leave it better than it was when we found it.

Once you have assurance and have chosen the purpose you believe God wants you to fulfill in life, it is time to start focusing on your plan. Plans can change as goals are reevaluated, as you become more progressive toward reaching each goal.

Setting apart time to spend with God and meditation on His word is just a wish until you put it on your daily agenda. You may want to spend more time on the development of your family's strength. Until it is a goal and an agenda on your daily to do list, it is just a wish. You may have a political interest in the future of your country, but until you start contributing prayer and maybe financial contributions, as you are able, to that candidate, it is just a wish. If you have health goals, like staying in shape or losing weight, it is just a wish until it is on your daily to do list and followed through upon. In addition, there should be measurable benchmarks along the way until you get to your health goals.

The career path you wish to achieve is only a dream without goals and benchmarks to measure progress. It is the same with finances, financial planning for retirement and investments need to be planned with benchmark goals to measure progress until goals are reached.

CHAPTER XI

"LEGACY"

"The memory of the righteous is blessed, but the name of the wicked will rot." Proverbs 10:7, NKJV.

Do not limit God - Dream big and go for it. "Family and Others" remember those who dream big and accomplish big. Family remembers the average and mediocre person. Choices in the areas we discussed in this book will determine the legacy you leave. Proverbs speaks of legacy this way, Proverbs, "A man will be commended according to his wisdom, but he who is of a perverse heart will be despised." Proverbs 12: 8, NKJV. Aimlessness is despised wisdom, think about it! How you will be remembered is defined by how you live now. Nabal, just days before his death, was commended for his wisdom. "Now therefore, know and consider what you will do, for harm is determined against our master and against all his household. For he is such a scoundrel that one cannot speak to him." 1 Samuel 25: 17, NKJV. His name rotted - some thought good riddance. His wisdom was folly.

How we are going to be remembered on this earth after we are gone? Timothy says by our works. "Some men's sins are clearly evident, preceding them to judgment, but those of some men follow later. Likewise, the good works of some are

clearly evident, and those that are otherwise cannot be hidden."
1 Timothy 5: 24 – 25, NKJV.

Let us live as to make people sad we left - not glad we are
gone! God Bless and it has been my hope and prayer that this
little book inspires and comforts you to evolve in this new life
and be all you can be to the glory of God. Amen.

Twenty years from now you will be more disappointed by
the things that you didn't do more than by the ones you did do.
So, throw off the bowlines. Sail away from the safe harbor. Catch
the trade winds in your sails. Explore, dream, and discover *(Live
and conquer life for God)*.

- Mark Twain – *(Emphasis Mine)*

Therefore we also pray always for you that our God would
count you worthy of this calling, and fulfill all the good pleasure
of His goodness and the work of faith with power, that the name
of our Lord Jesus Christ may be glorified in you, and you in
Him, according to the grace of our God and the Lord Jesus
Christ. 2 Thessalonians 1: 11 -12, NKJV.

"The Lord bless you and keep you; The Lord make His
face shine upon you, and be gracious to you, The Lord lift up
His countenance upon you, and give you peace." Numbers 6:
24 – 26, NKJV.

Amen, Pastor Jim